Patsy Kanter + Steven Leinwand

developing numerical fluency

Making Numbers, Facts, and Computation Meaningful

HEINEMANN

Portsmouth, NH

Heinemann

361 Hanover Street

Portsmouth, NH 03801–3912

www.heinemann.com

Offices and agents throughout the world

The authors and publisher wish to thank those who have generously given permission to reprint borrowed material:

Excerpts from the Common Core State Standards. Copyright © 2010. National Governors Association Center for Best Practices and Council of Chief State School Officers. All rights reserved.

(continued on page xiv)

Cataloging-in-Publication Data is on file at the Library of Congress.

ISBN: 978-0-325-09312-3

Editor: Katherine Bryant

Production: Victoria Merecki

Cover and text designs: Monica Ann Crigler

Typesetter: Shawn Girsberger

Author photos: Pableaux Johnson (Kanter) and HMH/Kevin Wolf (Leinwand)

Manufacturing: Steve Bernier

Printed in the United States of America on acid-free paper

22 21 20 19 CG 2 3 4 5

Dedicated to Ernie and to Ann.
They keep us centered,
honest, and very happy.

Contents

Introduction

We have been teaching mathematics to children and to their teachers since the early 1980s. We encourage teachers to see the power of student discourse to foster engagement, models to support visualization, contexts to connect the mathematics to the real world of children, and alternative strategies to effectively differentiate. We have seen how these strategies, all of which have the support of a growing body of research and the wisdom of good practice, have changed the trajectory of student learning of mathematics. These same strategies apply directly to the challenge of ensuring the development of numerical fluency in all elementary school students.

Defining Numerical Fluency

Join us on the rug with twenty-two second graders. "Ready?" we ask. "Turn and tell your partner how much eight plus nine is." After about ten seconds we add, "Call out what you said to, or heard from, your partner when we point to you." We hear a chorus of "seventeen" with a "sixteen" or an "eighteen" here and there, and even a stray "one" mixed in. "Great. Again, with your partner, use words, numbers, or pictures on your whiteboards to convince the class that eight plus nine really is seventeen." Here is what we often hear:

> *I knew that eight plus eight is sixteen, and because nine is one more than eight, eight plus nine has to be seventeen.*

> *We decomposed the eight into seven and one and added the one to nine to get ten and then seven more for seventeen in all.*

> *I drew eight tallies on top and nine tallies on the bottom and counted them all to get seventeen.*

> *I did a similar but different way by adding one to the nine and taking one away from the eight so that eight plus nine was the same as seven plus ten or seventeen.*

> *We used a double too, but we thought that since nine plus nine was eighteen, eight plus nine had to be one less or seventeen.*

> *I thought of ten-frames and since eight is a ten with two holes and nine is a ten with one hole, eight plus nine had to be ten plus ten or twenty minus the three holes, or seventeen.*

This is when and why teaching mathematics is such a joy! This is a small example of what we consider to be teaching that develops fluency and students who can demonstrate that fluency. Even incorrect answers or explanations are just as valuable as these correct answers, as we hear students argue about who is right, why they disagree, and then often correct themselves.

What Fluency Is

In the K–5 *Common Core State Standards for Mathematics* (National Governors Association 2010), the word "fluently" appears only *seven* times:

- Grade K: Fluently add and subtract within 5.
- Grade 2: Fluently add and subtract within 20 using mental strategies.

- Grade 2: Fluently add and subtract within 100 using strategies based on place value, properties of operations, and/or the relationship between addition and subtraction.

- Grade 3: Fluently multiply and divide within 100, using strategies such as the relationship between multiplication and division or properties of operations.

- Grade 3: Fluently add and subtract within 1000, using strategies and algorithms based on place value, properties of operations, and/or the relationship between addition and subtraction.

- Grade 4: Fluently add and subtract multi-digit whole numbers, using the standard algorithm.

- Grade 5: Fluently multiply and divide whole numbers, using the standard algorithm.

> We disagree with one point in these standards: the notion of *the* "standard algorithm" is one of very few glaring errors in the Common Core and needs to be read and implemented as *a* "standard algorithm" that encourages the teaching of alternatives that are much more accessible to many students. We will discuss this more in Chapters 6 and 9.

Note the relationship between fluency and *mental strategies,* and between fluency and *place value* and *properties.* Fluency is tied directly to *conceptual understanding* of numbers, place value, and operations, not simply to rote memorization of procedures. As the National Council of Teachers of Mathematics said in *Principles to Actions*:

> Fluency is not a simple idea. Being fluent means that students are able to choose flexibly among methods and strategies to solve contextual and mathematical problems, they understand and are able to explain their approaches, and they are able to produce accurate answers efficiently. Fluency builds from initial exploration and discussion of number concepts to using informal reasoning strategies based on meaning and properties of the operations. (NCTM 2014, 42)

Based on all this research, we argue that:

- ▣ Numerical fluency is about understanding, not memorization.
- ▣ Numerical fluency is supported by fingers, pictures, and all sorts of materials—that is, multiple representations that best fit individual students' conceptions.
- ▣ Numerical fluency develops when students communicate their understandings and construct and share their strategies.
- ▣ Numerical fluency is developed much more through engaging tasks and activities with rich questions and student discourse than through endless practice with mindless "get-the-answer" worksheets.

What Fluency Is Not

Unfortunately, this broader conception of fluency is very different from what we find in many classrooms and helps to explain why so many students struggle with mathematics in elementary school. We often hear a range of definitions that neither we, nor the research, support:

- ▣ Fluency is instantaneous recall.
- ▣ Fluent students do not have to use their fingers.
- ▣ Fluency is a good indicator of a student's mathematical ability.
- ▣ Fluency is correctly identifying the answers to 100 facts in a very short time.
- ▣ Fluency is the ability to quickly and accurately add, subtract, multiply, and divide with pencil and paper.

These are the deeply held beliefs and mindsets that guide instruction in too many classrooms. It is our conviction that these beliefs are counterproductive and even very destructive for many of our students.

The Challenge: Teaching in Ways We Were Not Taught

As we travel around the country, we are excited to see that fluency has been elevated in school-based discussions and has drawn the attention of many teachers. Done correctly, the development of numerical fluency empowers students and helps them develop lifelong understanding and confidence. Done wrongly or poorly, we deprive students of mathematical empowerment and send them messages that severely undermine their long-term mathematical development. We see exceptional teachers who are fully committed to teaching conceptually, but who still resort to speed tests because they see no alternatives. We see good mathematics programs that fail to give teachers structures for instruction or effective strategies that develop fluent mathematicians. And the questions we get remain essentially the same:

- "How do I teach number facts so that students know their facts with fluency?"
- "How do I help students who only want to follow rules that they obviously don't understand to compute accurately, efficiently and with confidence?"
- "Why do my students have such difficulty estimating sums, differences, products, and quotients?"

We believe that the core of the problem is that most teachers today learned mathematics as routines and procedures. When asked for the sum of eight and five, they have no problem answering "thirteen," and explaining that this is simply a "fact I have memorized." But when asked to apply this knowledge to 38 + 5— clearly 30 more than 13, or 43, calculated with elementary place value understandings—these same teachers ask for pencil and paper and resort to procedures including "and carry the one." These teachers (and many of our students) do not have numerical fluency. They know their facts, but have not acquired the critical ability or disposition to think and reason numerically in ways that represent the fluency called for by the Common Core. Simply put, the facts are essential, but not enough.

In addition, many teachers are the products of instruction that made regular use of timed tests of facts. They struggle to find other, more effective, ways to build students' fluency. Unfortunately, this keeps the focus on rote memory and speed, not on understanding and the powerful thinking and visualization strategies that undergird true fluency. As a result, far too many students, early in their mathematical careers, learn that mathematics is arithmetic and that arithmetic is the mindless memorization and regurgitation of facts and procedures that don't have to make sense and that don't relate to the bigger aspects of conceptual understanding.

Instead, we envision teaching that starts with that conceptual understanding first, and builds fluency from it. Figure I.1 summarizes what this kind of teaching looks like—what teachers and students are doing when this kind of work is going on.

Build procedural fluency from conceptual understanding (NCTM 2014, 47–48)

What are *teachers* doing?	What are *students* doing?
● Providing students with opportunities to use their own reasoning strategies and methods for solving problems	● Making sure that they understand and can explain the mathematical basis for the procedures that they are using
● Asking students to discuss and explain why the procedures that they are using work to solve particular problems	● Demonstrating flexible use of strategies and methods while reflecting on which procedures seem to work best for specific types of problems
● Connecting student-generated strategies and methods to more efficient procedures as appropriate	● Determining whether specific approaches generalize to a broad class of problems
● Using visual models to support students' understanding of general methods	● Striving to use procedures appropriately and efficiently
● Providing students with opportunities for distributed practice of procedures	

Figure I.1 *Teacher and student actions to build procedural fluency*

There is an unacceptable chasm between traditional mathematics instruction, that rarely works for more than one-third of our students, and this kind of mathematics instruction, that truly empowers nearly all students.

Our Goals for This Book

Our goals in the chapters that follow are to provide a broad range of ideas, techniques, activities, and strategies for converting these teacher and student actions into ongoing classroom practices. The questions we pose, and answer, in this book include:

- How can fluency be developed more effectively?
- What specific strategies and techniques can teachers use to develop numerical fluency in all students?
- Why are these approaches so important for building a stronger foundation for all mathematical learning?

To answer these questions we begin by defining numerical fluency in terms of what we believe it is, and, as importantly, what it is *not*, trying to sweep aside a range of misconceptions about fluency and how best to develop it. Upon the definitional foundation laid out above, we start in Chapter 1 with a set of nine pivotal understandings that undergird all of our instructional work to develop numerical fluency. We believe that these understandings form a powerful hierarchy of skills and concepts that help teachers diagnose diverse readiness; differentiate as needed; and place instruction, reteaching, and reinforcement along a common continuum from understanding parts and wholes to a mature sense of place value and operations.

But as we have learned from both the *Principles and Standards for School Mathematics* (NCTM 2000) and the *Common Core State Standards for Mathematics* (National Governors Association 2010), student processes or practices are as important as, and intertwined with, the mathematical content itself. Accordingly, we turn in Chapter 2 to six critical processes for the development of numerical fluency that characterize all effective instruction: contextualizing, constructing, representing, visualizing, verbalizing, and justifying. These six processes, in combination with the ten pivotal understandings, create the weft and warp of our numerical fluency tapestry. Then in Chapter 3 we propose and describe a set of classroom structures that support classroom instruction demonstrating this tapestry of numerical fluency.

Chapters 4, 5, and 6 apply this framework to the development of addition and subtraction fluency, and Chapters 7, 8, and 9 apply it to the development of multiplication and division fluency. Each chapter identifies and describes a set of big ideas that unify good instruction, and provides a range of examples and vignettes drawn from our classroom experiences. Finally, in Chapters 10 and 11 we offer suggestions for some easy-to-implement schoolwide activities and resources and the professional development and collaboration that are required to ensure that it is the entire elementary school, and not just individual teachers, that shares the responsibility for developing numerical confidence, joy and fluency in every student.

PART ONE

Building Understanding of Numerical Fluency

Chapter 1

Nine Pivotal Understandings for Numerical Fluency

The teaching practices delineated in *Principles to Actions* (NCTM 2014, 42) call on us to "build procedural fluency from conceptual understanding." But the question teachers face is what constitutes this "foundation of conceptual understanding" that enables students to "become skillful in using procedures flexibly as they solve contextual and mathematical problems?" We believe that teachers must embrace nine pivotal understandings to support the development of numerical fluency in all students. We have found that while none are gatekeepers to, or more important than, any of the others, when viewed across the elementary grades these understandings progress from foundational notions of parts and wholes that undergird the development of fluency in grades K and 1 to a mature understanding of place value that undergirds estimation and computation with larger numbers in grades 4 and 5. In this chapter we describe and give examples of each of these understandings. In the remainder of this book, we model how these understandings play out in the development of numerical fluency across the grades.

These nine pivotal understandings are:

1. Everything begins with counting.

2. All quantities are composed of parts and wholes, meaning that all whole numbers greater than 1 can be decomposed into smaller whole numbers. (In fact, *all* numbers can be decomposed into smaller numbers, but we limit our focus here only to whole numbers.)

3. Acquisition of the language of the four operations (joining, separating, sharing, combining, comparing, each group, groups of, more, more than, less, less than, etc.) must precede the learning of facts.

4. Powerful properties of operations reduce memory load and contribute to numerical fluency.

5. Facility using 5 and 10 in computation underpins numerical fluency.

6. Deeply understanding that 9 and 10 − 1 are the same number supports numerical fluency with a range of so-called "hard" facts.

7. Multiplication by 2, 3, 5, and 10 are the foundation for fluency with all multiplication and division facts.

8. The notion of balance or equivalence in equations and the meaning of the equal sign are fundamental to comprehending operations and algebraic thinking.

9. Place value understanding is essential to build fluency with larger numbers.

Pivotal Understanding 1: *Everything Begins with Counting*

It is not uncommon for people, including teachers, to think that first children can count to 10, then to 20 conquering the teen numbers, and then to 100, and at that point counting becomes irrelevant to mathematical development. In fact, counting on takes us to addition, counting back takes us to subtraction, skip-counting takes us to multiplication, and skip-counting backward gets us close to division. That is why "Can you solve it by counting?" can be such an appropriate question and strategy before numbers get too large. Teachers support fluency by asking students to:

> *Count on by ones starting at 15.*
>
> *Count back by ones starting at 35.*
>
> *Count on by twos starting at 22.*
>
> *Count back by tens starting at 145.*
>
> *Skip-count by sixes starting at 42.*
>
> *Skip-count backward by eights starting at 80.*

Counting forward and backward then expands to include explicit attention to the relationships that underlie counting, such as:

What do you know about counting numbers forward? (They are all one more than the one before.)

What about the numbers you say when you count backward? (They are all one less than the one before.)

What can you tell me about this sequence: 0, 2, 4, 6, 8, 10, 12, 14, 16, 18, 20? (They are all groups of two, or two more than the last one.) Then, why do we call these even numbers? Also will 32 be in this sequence? How do you know?

What can you tell me about this sequence: 1, 3, 5, 7, 9, 11, 13, 15, 17, 19?

What can you tell me about this sequence: 0, 3, 6, 9, 12, 15, 18, 21?

What can you tell me about this sequence: 1, 4, 7, 10, 13, 16, 19, 22?

What can you tell me about this sequence: 0, 5, 10, 15, 20, 25?

Pivotal Understanding 2: *All Quantities Are Composed of Parts and Wholes*

Addition, subtraction, multiplication, and division are mathematical shorthand for dealing with parts and wholes. Sometimes the parts and wholes are addends and sums that are related by addition or subtraction. Other times, the parts and wholes are factors and multiples related by multiplication or division. Sometimes the parts are equal and sometimes they are not. Sometimes there is a fractional part of a whole. These parts can be put together and taken away in a variety of ways, leading to the various operations. Understanding what the whole is, what the parts are, how they are related, and what might be missing in a particular problem are all critical aspects of numerical fluency. These ideas are not obvious to young children and emerge gradually from experiences with numbers and operations.

Composing and Decomposing Numbers

Very young children must develop an understanding that the numerals they say and write represent quantities that can be counted or measured. These quantities can be broken into parts or remain as wholes. Whether the parts are equal or unequal, they will always recombine to make the same whole. Being able to conceptualize all whole numbers this way provides children with information to tell stories about joining and separating parts and using parts to make larger and smaller numbers. All understanding of operations, whether addition, subtraction, multiplication, or division, grows from these early experiences composing and decomposing numbers. Not only are these understandings essential for developing number sense and numerical fluency, they are the critical precursors to all algebraic reasoning.

How do we begin to help our students develop a full understanding of parts, wholes, composing, and decomposing? Pre-kindergartners might look at three pencils. If you hold one in your hand, two are on the table. If you hold two in your hand, one is on the table, and if you pick up all three, none are on the table. If you put them into three groups, there is one pencil in each group. These early experiences and the talk that accompanies them help young children develop understanding of parts and wholes. As their understanding develops, they can tell all the different ways to make five counters using some red and some blue counters. From first grade on, knowing all the ways to make the numbers to 10 is critical.

Figure 1.1 *Arrangements of six*

Look at the creativity displayed when first graders are asked to color in exactly six squares in a three by three grid (see Figure 1.1). Now consider how this activity grows into $6 + 3 = 9$, $3 + 6 = 9$, $9 - 3 = 6$, and $9 - 6 = 3$. Note also how each grid is uniquely colored. These students are not just coloring for fun; they are making sense of decomposing 9 into 6 and 3 in concrete and visually clear ways.

The Importance of Small Numbers

Comfort and confidence with small numbers is the cornerstone of learning "number facts." Students must be able to automatically decompose the numbers 3–6. Students must also be able to *subitize* small numbers; that is, be able to tell "how many" without counting every object in a small group. Most children can quickly identify sets up to five without counting. They then learn to identify larger numbers quickly by identifying their parts, such as seeing six as groups of three and three or two and four.

But it all begins with one and two, where one and one more must be two and where one less than two must be one, because all subsequent addition and subtraction is merely adding or taking away more ones. Over time children accumulate a broad array of knowledge about one and two, which contributes to their number sense repertoire and aids in problem solving.

Here are some "noticings" students have about the number 1 as they progress through elementary school:

> *One is the first number I say when I count to one hundred.* (Grades K–1)

> *One more is one more than the last number when I count.* (Grade 1)

> *One less than is the number that came before the number when I count.* (Grades 1–2)

> *One is what makes nine a ten!* (Grades 1–2)

> *One when added to an even number makes the number odd, and one when added to an odd number makes it even.* (Grades 2–3)

> *One when divided into parts yields a fractional part, such as one divided by four is one-fourth, but twelve divided by one gives one in each group.* (Grades 4–5)

> *One is not an even number or a prime number but it is a factor of all other numbers.* (Grades 4–5)

And here are some wonderful observations about two to remind us where "Turn and tell your partner something amazing about the number two" can lead a class of fourth graders:

> *Two is the smallest even number and the only prime even number.*

> *When two is added to an even number you always get another even number, but when two is added to an odd number you get another odd number.*

> *Two is the group of things we count by most easily, like ears and eyes and the animals on Noah's ark, which are all counted two, four, six, eight, etc.*

> *Two is half of four, two and three more are five, three twos are six, and two plus two plus two plus one are seven!*

> Two doubles in multiplication to become a four-times fact and that
> doubles to make an eight-times fact.
>
> Two is what makes eight a ten, eighteen a twenty, twenty-eight a thirty, and
> so on.

We return to this pivotal understanding in greater depth in Chapter 4.

Pivotal Understanding 3: *Acquiring the Language of Operations Before Learning Facts*

Understanding of quantitative, symbolic, and abstract number sentences and equations needs to be balanced with the more verbal language of operations and arithmetic situations. That is why explaining in words, acting out, and storytelling are all essential strategies for developing operation sense and numerical fluency. (We'll discuss these strategies more in the next chapter.)

Consider asking students to find the total cost of a twenty-five cent pen and a fifteen-cent pencil. Many can quickly tell us "forty cents." But it is the questions "What operation did you use?" and "Why did you add?" that stimulate the connections between language and facts and between situations and operations. When class discussion produces the following responses, we can see that the links between language and actions are growing stronger.

> I added because we had to put two things together.
>
> I added because the pen was twenty-five cents and the pencil was more.
>
> I added because we had to combine the two prices.

Actions Determine Operations

When solving straightforward word problems involving the four operations, we need to ask such questions as:

> Are we combining or separating?
>
> Are we comparing two quantities?
>
> Are we sharing or combining?
>
> Do we have equal groups or groups of equal amounts?

Thus, it is the language of these actions that determines which operations to use to write number sentences and solve problems. In *Children's Mathematics, Cognitively Guided Instruction*, Tom Carpenter and his colleagues (1999) have identified and classified the language of addition and subtraction, multiplication and division. This work is the basis of categories used in the appendix to the *Common Core State Standards for Mathematics* (National Governors Association 2010) and is included in the Appendix to this book (see page 165). Using these classifications to tell and act out stories will give children a firm understanding of operations and how to connect the equations that represent the relationship.

A good example is subtraction. There are several different situations in which experienced solvers might use subtraction: taking away, finding a missing addend, or comparison. While you could use subtraction to solve all of them, the action involved in each situation is different.

> *Taking away:* **11 peaches were in the basket. I ate 3. How many peaches are in the basket now?**
>
> **11 − 3 = ?**
>
> *Missing addend:* **11 cherries were in the bowl. I ate some. Then there were 3 cherries left. How many cherries did I eat?**
>
> **11 − ? = 3**
>
> *Comparison:* **Shelly has 11 checkmarks. James has 3. How many more does Shelly have than James?**
>
> **11 − 3 = ?**

Many teachers feel that "word problems" are the most difficult part of their early mathematics instruction, often recalling how word problems were for themselves as learners. However, using storytelling and contextualizing along with the language of operations before equation writing and finding answers allows students to see word problems as natural parts of mathematics.

Pivotal Understanding 4: *Properties of Operations*

Properties of operations are commonly considered among the most boring topics in the mathematics curriculum. Lessons devoted just to naming them may certainly qualify! But *using* the properties and helping students understand how and why they work and how much easier they make the learning of mathematics are much more powerful.

Commutative and Associative Properties

A student who understands the commutative properties of addition and multiplication—the "order of the addends or the factors doesn't matter" property—significantly reduces the challenge of learning facts. Instead of being overwhelmed by 121 addition facts, students use the commutative property to think, for example, that $9 + 4$ is the same as $4 + 9$, thus reducing the number of unique addition facts to only 66. This also applies—and is even more important—when learning multiplication facts. As we'll discuss in Part Two, helping students recognize how many plus zero, plus one, plus two, and doubles facts they already know significantly reduces the sense of being overwhelmed by the idea that there are just too many facts to learn them all. A deep understanding of this property helps students master the additional insight that while addition and multiplication *are* commutative, subtraction and division are *not* commutative.

Understanding the properties of commutativity and associativity can help children decompose and recompose numbers more easily and in ways that develop greater fluency. A student faced with $7 + 3$ can decompose the 7 and think of the problem as $(5 + 2) + 3$, and, even without naming it, use the associative property to recombine the numbers as $5 + (2 + 3)$, or $5 + 5$. This kind of decomposition and recombination is key to developing fluency.

Distributive Property

Similarly, the distributive property supports the development of multiplication and division facts. Students who struggle with 6×7 can conceptualize this fact as $(3 \times 7) + (3 \times 7)$ which many find easier to remember. When multiplying 20×21, they can use the distributive property to multiply $20 \times (10 + 11)$, leading to $(20 \times 10) + (20 \times 11) = 200 + 220 = 420$.

Combining all of these properties enables students to fluently calculate the product of 6 and 20. Our students can often multiply 6 by 20 with pencil and paper, but numerical fluency enables them to see the 20 as 10×2 and almost seamlessly convert 6×20 to $6 \times (10 \times 2)$ to $(6 \times 2) \times 10$ or 12×10 or 120! All because of the properties of operations.

Inverse Operations and Fact Families

Although not technically a formal property, the understanding that if $a + b = c$, then $c - a = b$ and $c - b = a$ is what creates fact families and enables students to think about addition when they are subtracting. When we work with the always challenging multiplication and division facts, relying on the commutative property and fact families enables a student who fully understands that $6 \times 7 = 42$ to be able to fluently identify 7×6, $42 \div 6$, and $42 \div 7$.

To achieve a full and intuitive understanding of properties, children need to have frequent practice, which encourages the flexibility and facility to use these properties naturally; this practice comes in the forms of problem solving, game playing, and explaining one's thinking (as we will discuss more in Part Two).

Pivotal Understanding 5: *Using 5 and 10*

Ten is the pivotal number in our system. We have ten digits—0 to 9—in our number system, our place value system is based on 10, and all numbers beyond 10 demand an understanding that ten 1s are *unitized* into one 10. Therefore 10, and its relationship with every other number, demands focused attention, understanding, and practice.

Likewise, five is the largest possible quantity that most people can visualize without counting or using a strategic configuration. Moreover, children are regularly exposed to applications of five: days of the school week on a calendar, minutes on a clock, a tally, fingers and toes on one hand or foot, pennies in a nickel. Because 5 plus 5 equals 10, and 5 is half of 10, 5 and its interactions with 10 have many implications in numerical fluency. That is why using five- and ten-frames, grids, tally marks, and fingers are so valuable for reinforcing understanding of these key relationships.

Mastery of sums to 5 and 5 + numbers, that is, $5 + 1$, $5 + 2$, $5 + 3$, etc., is critical for developing fluency. Knowing that $5 + 2 = 7$ and $5 + 4 = 9$ and $5 + 5 = 10$, when combined with an understanding of properties, can help students figure out harder facts like $7 + 9$: $(5 + 2) + (5 + 4) = (5 + 5) + (4 + 2) = 10 + 6 = 16$.

A good example of the power of fives is seen in having two children hold up their hands to add 6 and 6, as shown in Figure 1.2. First, the children model six as a five and one more. As they move their hands together, they put five and five

Figure 1.2 *Showing 6s with fingers*

together to make ten, and one and one together to make two, or twelve in all. This is obviously the same as adding a nickel and one penny and a nickel and one penny to get two nickels and two pennies or one dime and two pennies.

Pivotal Understanding 6: *9 and 10 – 1 Are the Same Number*

Nine and ten share a special relationship that supports fluency. Nine is a large quantity that is not easily visualized or conceptualized. However when nine is viewed—with fingers or with ten frames—as one less than ten, it becomes much easier to visualize and to use with all four operations. For example, it is easier and more efficient for students to add 10 and subtract 1 than to struggle to add 9. When wrestling with 38 + 9, the power of fluency enables students to think, "38 and 10 is 48, but I added one too many so the sum must be 47." Similarly, it is often easier for students to multiply by 10 and then subtract when multiplying by 9. We know that 9 × 6 = 54 is one of the more challenging facts for many students.

While we're focusing on the power of 9 as 10 − 1, it is worth noting that 9 is also intriguing to many students. Consider the fascinating patterns in adding 9 and multiplying by 9 shown in the charts below. Consider posting one or both charts and asking students:

How many patterns can you find here?

Can you explain why each of these patterns occurs?

	+9				×9	
1	+ 9	= 10		1	× 9	= 9
2	+ 9	= 11		2	× 9	= 18
3	+ 9	= 12		3	× 9	= 27
4	+ 9	= 13		4	× 9	= 36
5	+ 9	= 14		5	× 9	= 45
6	+ 9	= 15		6	× 9	= 54
7	+ 9	= 16		7	× 9	= 63
8	+ 9	= 17		8	× 9	= 72
9	+ 9	= 18		9	× 9	= 81

However, fluency leads to thinking that 10 sixes is 60, so 9 sixes must be one fewer 6, or 54.

Similarly, when using tallies to record data, children gain experience recognizing 9 as five clustered tally marks with four left over and then see that one more is needed to make 10. Also, time on a clock shows 9 as one less than 10 hours or minutes, and most commonly, putting up nine fingers means showing one less than ten (see Figure 1.3).

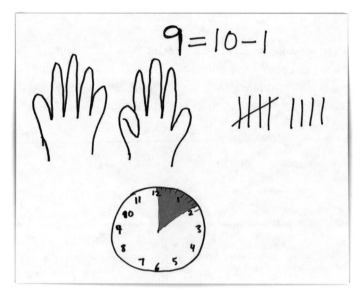

Figure 1.3 *Different examples of 9 as 1 less than 10*

Pivotal Understanding 7: *Multiplication by 2, 3, 5, and 10*

Teachers have known for generations that multiplying by 2, 3, 5, and 10 are often easier to master than multiplying by 4, 6, 7, 8, and 9. The mastery of these facts also supports the learning and mastery of all the remaining multiplication facts. Too often, this hierarchy of facts is lost in a textbook program that essentially equates products with 3, 5, 7, and 9, depriving students of the opportunity to build fluency on the backs of easier facts. For example, when students understand that 6×7 is just 3×7 twice, they combine a fact they know ($3 \times 7 = 21$) with addition to fluently understand and remember that 6×7 must be 42. And then there are other students who understand that 6×7 is simply 5×7, or 35, and 7 more. Before dismissing this reasoning as a far too complicated strategy that justifies just memorizing that $6 \times 7 = 42$, ask teachers in a faculty meeting exactly what their brain is thinking when they move from 6×7 to 42. You may be surprised how often the factors 2, 3, 5, and 10 are used!

We know that multiplication problems can be solved by repeated addition, and division by repeated subtraction, but this is not efficient and therefore not fluency. That is, adding a number to itself over and over is only a strategy to derive the answer, not a measure of mathematical literacy. What *is* important is the understanding that repeated addition works because multiplication involves equal groups replicated some number of times. That is, 5×7 is conceptualized as five replications of a group of seven, or seven replications of a group of five. Similarly, moving beyond repeated subtraction, dividing means creating groups that each have the same quantity (how many groups?) or creating some number of equal-sized groups (how many in each group?). We return to these ideas in greater detail in Part Three.

Multiplying by 2

Many teachers and students find that multiplying by 2 seems very easy and either race through it, jumping right to memorization, or skip it altogether. We are asked, "Don't students simply skip-count by two or know their doubles?" However, seeing groups of equal quantities serves as a powerful link between multiplication and those doubles children learned in addition. In addition, focusing on products of 2 also helps children to visualize the relationship between how many total objects are in six groups of two and how many are in each group if twelve items are split into two equal groups, both of which are key prerequisite understandings for division. What works reasonably easily with 2 becomes the foundation and reference for moving on to 3s, 5s, and other multiples. Figure 1.4 is a poster created by third graders that reminds us of the importance of multiplying by 2.

Multiplying by 3

Products of 3 are another significant and accessible group of numbers with which to have fluency. "Two threes

How multiples of 2 help us

• We know odd from even
• Twos become fours and eights
• Help us factor any even number
• Help us multiply with 20
• When we divide an odd number by 2 there is always 1 left over
• We can count faster by 2s
• Two groups of odd numbers make an even number

Figure 1.4 *What we know about 2*

are six" and "one more than three is four" are relationships that can support the learning of multiples of 6 and 4. Products of 3s have an interesting pattern, alternating odd and even, and the digits of any multiple of 3 will always add to a multiple of 3.

Multiplying by 5 and 10

As noted in Pivotal Understanding 6, 5s and 10s are also very important to developing number sense. Building on the fact most children are comfortable counting by 5—often in singsong fashion—teachers can connect this skip-counting to products. For children for whom using products of 3 to build products of 4 and 6 does not work well, products of 5 are an excellent alternative: 6×4 is the same as 5×4 plus 4. Because 5 doubles to 10, a good strategy for multi-digit multiplication by 5 is to multiply by 10 and then take half.

It is critical that students understand that multiplying by 10 does not just mean writing a zero at the end of a number, but that the amount is increased by a factor of 10. Being told "put a zero in the ones place on the second row" when multiplying multi-digit numbers, without understanding why, leaves many students confused. In addition, the phase "add a zero" when multiplying by 10 tends to wreak havoc when we move to multiplying decimals, since appending a zero does not change a decimal's value.

Pivotal Understanding 8: *Equivalence in Equations and the Meaning of the Equal Sign*

Ask first, second, and third graders what number goes in the blank in: $3 + 4 = \underline{\hspace{0.5cm}} + 2$. Many teachers are flabbergasted at how many students say 7! These students view the equal sign as a "show the answer" sign, not as a symbol of equivalence. This is why it is not surprising that students struggle mightily with missing addend and factor problems ($4 + \underline{\hspace{0.5cm}} = 13$ or $4 \times \underline{\hspace{0.5cm}} = 36$).

We emphasize this pivotal idea of equivalence because it is a prerequisite understanding for creating and using equations and number sentences. For example, consider the following scenario. First graders are wrestling with the following situation:

There are 6 children on the bus; some are boys and some are girls.

Sarah says there must be 3 girls and 3 boys.

Is Sarah correct or not? How do you know?

Look at how this scenario supports joining and separating numbers, number fact fluency, and also the notions of balance and equivalence in number sentences. One student says that Sarah is correct because three boys and three girls is the same as six children because $3 + 3 = 6$. Another student proposes that there could also be four girls and two boys. This leads to "what are all the combinations of boys and girls on the bus and how can we present this in a table and with number sentences?" Each such combination, although using different numbers, is equivalent to 6.

Balance and equivalence, as well as common misconceptions, all surface during examination and discussion of the following True/False statements:

$3 + 4 = 8$ True or False? Why or why not?

$3 + 1 = 30 + 1$ True or False? Why or why not?

$10 - 7 = 6 - 3$ True or False? Why or why not?

$3 + 4 = 43$ True or False? Why or why not?

$40 - 30 = 10 + 0$ True or False? Why or why not?

Pivotal Understanding 9: *Place Value Understanding*

While facts to 10 are pivotal for small number fluency, understanding place value is pivotal for larger number computation. For example, facts establish that $3 + 4 = 7$, but it is place value understanding that establishes that $30 + 40 = 70$. Similarly, facts establish that 4×7 is 28, but it is place value that helps us understand that 4×70 is 280. As we argue in Part Three, fluency with multiplying by multiples of 10 and 100 and 1000, combined with fact fluency, underlies nearly all numerical fluency with multiplication and division.

For an example of how to help students build place value understanding, see the video at

hein.pub/NumericalFluency

(click on Companion Resources)

Consider, for example, a student calculating the sum $56 + 27 =$ _____. Think of all the key understandings that are needed here:

1. $50 + 20 = 70$ so an answer less than 70 is not reasonable.
2. $6 + 7$ creates another ten with 3 left over.
3. Adding 1 ten to 5 tens and 2 tens is 8 tens, or 80.
4. And the 3 that remains represents 3 ones, not 3 tens.

The answer is 83 but our job as teachers must be to expect and understand why so many children think that entirely correct answers—all based on common place value misunderstandings—are 73, 93, or 31!

As students move from two- to three-digit numbers and beyond, the continued need for place value understanding is compounded. For example, a student doing the problem 116 divided by 3 has many opportunities to demonstrate core place value understandings.

> The answer will be at least 30 because $3 \times 30 = 90$ and $3 \times 40 = 120$.
>
> If I take 30 groups of 3 out, I am left with 26. That is an easy problem.
>
> 26 divided by 3 is 8 remainder 2.
>
> Add the 8 to the 30 and you get 38 remainder 2.

These nine pivotal ideas provide a cognitive foundation upon which children become numerically fluent. It should be clear at this point that these understandings cannot be taught in only a lesson or two. Rather, they must be integrated into ongoing activities and conversations and infused throughout instruction. In the next chapter we'll look at the six processes with which students need to engage for that instruction to be as successful as possible.

Chapter 2

Six Processes for Developing Numerical Fluency

As we noted in Chapter 1, students do not develop numerical fluency by memorization and regurgitation of rules. Rather, numerical fluency develops over time as students engage in active thinking and doing. They must strategize, reason, justify, and record and report on their thinking. Accordingly, the effective development of numerical fluency involves the use of a set of cognitive processes throughout mathematics, not just in one lesson or introductory lessons. When mathematics lessons are systematically planned and implemented with these six processes at the forefront, teachers maximize the chances of *all* students becoming numerically fluent and mathematically powerful!

The Six Processes

We have identified six processes that support the development of numerical fluency. Figure 2.1 summarizes the six processes in student-friendly terms and in more formal terms.

These processes are not unique to numerical fluency—in fact, the same processes are essential for the development of spatial sense, algebraic reasoning, and other big ideas in mathematics.

Formal cognitive process	Student-friendly terminology
Contextualizing	Storytelling
Physically constructing	Building
Representing graphically and symbolically	Drawing and using symbols
Visualizing	Seeing
Verbalizing	Describing what and how
Justifying	Discussing why

Figure 2.1 *Six processes for developing fluency*

1. **Contextualizing or Storytelling:** Understanding that life can be described mathematically is at the foundation of fluency. Equations exist because they are a shortcut to explain situations, look at reality, and make predictions. Too often we present equations without giving them context, leaving children without understanding and causing misconceptions.

2. **Physically Constructing or Building:** Children need to manipulate materials to develop an understanding of the action of operations, which is then extended to the visual or pictorial level and then to abstraction. Fluency demands multiple models and making connections between and among models.

3. **Representing Graphically and Symbolically or Drawing and Using Symbols:** Seeing and using models and relationships between models supports visual memory, building relationships, and mental fluency, and enhances long term memory. For many students, fluency depends on being able to visualize concepts in different ways and understand the relationships between these different representations.

4. **Visualizing or Seeing:** Children learn to visualize quantities and the relationships between them. As children accumulate a visual repertoire, their numerical fluency grows because they are able to "see" the mathematics in which they are engaged.

5. **Verbalizing or Describing What and How:** Understanding of operations is achieved when students describe and explain what they did with the materials that they manipulate and the pictures they draw. Students need

to describe the representations they create and how various representations are similar and different. Students should always be expected to describe the "what" and "how" of the mathematics they are learning, using informal and, gradually, formal mathematical language.

6. **Justifying or Discussing Why:** Discussing relationships and justifying solutions to problems is fundamental to developing metacognition and crucial to long-term fluency. Justifying answers the question "why?" and is one of the best ways to monitor the development of numerical fluency in students.

These six processes emerge from an expansion and elaboration on the core "concrete to representational to abstract" trajectory well-known to elementary teachers. All we've done is adapt "concrete" to become "construct" or "build" with physical materials, and focus "representational" on actual drawing and pictures. We also expand "representational" to include visualizing or abstracting the representations. And we add contextualizing in the form of storytelling, and replace "abstract" with verbalizing and justifying.

Fluency emerges from diverse experiences that link numbers and operations to contexts and familiar situations, and that provide students throughout their mathematical development with opportunities to construct, visualize, verbalize, and justify. Let's look at each of these processes in turn and see how each plays a critical role in supporting the development of numerical fluency.

These six processes are the essence of the differentiation needed to effectively teach mathematics. One student might make sense of subtracting in a context, while another needs to touch and feel the comparison of two qualities, while a third learns best by "talking through."

Contextualizing or Storytelling

Storytelling and contextualizing serve many purposes:

- Students develop a firmer understanding of the meaning of the operations by situating them in context. For instance, thinking about Sarah who had 4 apples and bought 3 more helps students understand the "adding on" meaning of addition.

■ Through storytelling, students have the chance to act out and visualize situations, providing the opportunity for two other important processes: constructing and visualizing (see more on these below). The context provides a starting point for students to construct and visualize the changes and relationships in the problem.

■ Asking students to create stories from numerical expressions helps students to make sense of numbers and operations and helps them make critical connections between abstract mathematics (3×7) and the real world (the area of a three cm. by seven cm. rectangle or the cost of three t-shirts that each costs $7).

■ And let's be honest. How many students really care about the product of 8 and 32, when the alternative is a YouTube video of the pandas in a zoo eating, accompanied by data like "eight pandas who each eat about thirty-two pounds of bamboo each day"? Such a context and the story about how many pounds of bamboo are needed to feed the pandas support engagement, smiles, and learning far more effectively than a workbook page of twenty naked multiplication problems where the goal is simply arriving at correct answers regardless of the depth of understanding.

What Contextualizing Looks Like

A kindergarten teacher writes on a flip chart (see Figure 2.2) and asks students to turn and tell their partners what they see. This question uses representations and verbalizations to stimulate various descriptions of the number 5 and is augmented by a discussion of how the three representations are the same and how they are different. But the critical link between the number 5 and the many contexts in which it appears emerges from the follow-up task posed to the students: "Stroll around our classroom with a partner and see how many places you can find this number, and how you know."

Students are contextualizing and connecting the abstraction of "five" as a numeral, a set of circles, and a word to their personal environments as they find and describe 5 on the clock, on the calendar in 5, 15, and 25, on the number line above the white board, with five books, five cubes, five fingers, or five

Figure 2.2 *A chart for 5*

markers. Needless to say, this ability is a critical precursor to operating with numbers and solving word problems.

Contextualizing also occurs when naked numbers (plain numbers with no context) are replaced with data or information, as in shifting 4 + 3 to four apples and three apples. We are great fans of using money, menus, price lists, and other familiar contexts as platforms for doing mathematics. And students contextualize every time we ask them to create their own story problems (as in Figure 2.3).

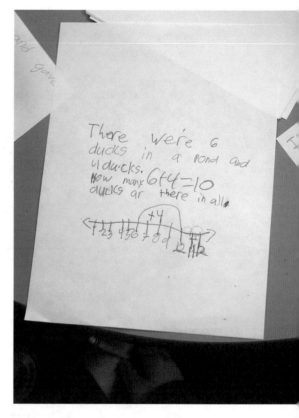

Figure 2.3 *Creating story problems with number lines*

Constructing or Building

Building with objects allows children a unique opportunity to create the structure of numbers and operations for themselves. No worksheet can teach a child place value as effectively as giving that child 153 beans, a place value mat, and fifteen cups to make tens. It is the process of grouping those ten beans into one cup that helps children understand how ten ones become one ten. This concept is fundamental, hard to grasp, rarely recognized as essential, and yet lies at the very core of understanding number relationships.

Similarly, young children's constructions help them create innate understandings. For example, when young children use number tiles to make 6 in different ways, with the rule that tiles must touch "full side to full side", they have the opportunity to explore many different ways to physically represent the number 6 (see Figure 2.4). Then, when students are asked to find how many different ways they can arrange the tiles, they need to determine that each configuration is unique. Out of these constructions, owned by the students, come insights that 2 and 4 make 6, 5 and 1 make 6, 3 and 3 make six, and so on, setting the stage for an understanding of part-part-whole relationships. This happens because the child built the arrangements and talked about what they built.

Constructing with concrete materials and objects is often a necessary prerequisite for drawing diagrams and pictures where it is more difficult to manipulate and rearrange the objects.

Figure 2.4 *Ways of arranging six square tiles*

What Constructing Looks Like

Tell a class of first graders about the child looking out of his or her bedroom window and seeing four birds in the branch of a tree. Next state with amazement that then the child looked down at the ground and saw three more birds! What seems so obvious—that there are seven birds in all—is very far from obvious to many children. Representing the four birds on the branch and the three birds on the ground with blocks or linking cubes is for many students a critical step in moving toward numerical fluency. Such activities are essential prerequisites for building an understanding of joining numbers, and can lead to drawings, visualizations, and fluently solving problems about joining and separating a group of four and a group of three. Note that here, as with nearly all of the examples we use, there is a natural reliance on more than one process, resulting in a combination of constructing, contextualizing, and verbalizing.

Representing Graphically and Symbolically or Drawing and Using Symbols

As students become comfortable using objects and materials to physically represent situations, we need them to be able to represent these mathematical situations using pictures, drawings, mathematical notation, and eventually equations, in addition to physical objects. Teachers often make the connection between constructing and drawing by asking students to replicate what they have already created with objects, but this time on paper with drawings. These representations constitute a pictorial and/or symbolic language that can and should help all students make sense of mathematics.

> Sharing different representations supports a deeper understanding of the power of multiple representations, because a representation that works for one student is unlikely to be the representation that works for all students.

When students move from drawings and pictures to representations like number sentences and equations, it is important to remember that equations are not merely tools to find answers, but are also symbolic mathematical representations that help to make mathematics so powerful. Drawings and other concrete and pictorial representations are not the end or the purpose, but rather key steps that connect to more abstract representations, like number sentences and equations (see Figure 2.5).

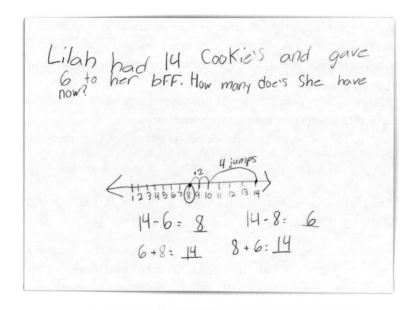

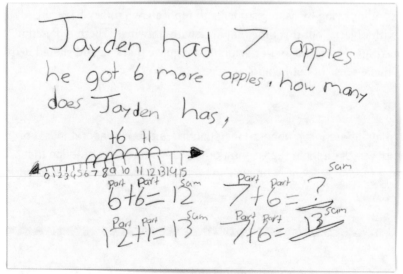

Figure 2.5 *Examples of combining abstract representations such as a number sentence and equations*

What Representing Looks Like

Representing includes understanding that signs for operations represent actions and that the equal sign means *equivalent* or *the same* and is *not* an operation or an action. First and second graders learn that the operation they see in put-together and add-on stories is represented with a + sign, and that what they do when comparing and taking apart or away is represented with a – sign. Likewise, students learn that finding the total of equal groups can be represented with multiplication symbols, and that splitting a whole into equal groups can be represented with division symbols.

Figure 2.6 shows some problems we've used with third graders that involve symbolic representations and help to build an understanding of operations and equality. Students who struggle with symbolic representations should be encouraged to use physical models to show the numbers before deciding whether to add or subtract.

Use +, –, = to make each of these a true number sentence.
1. 7   8   15
2. 10   7   3
3. 33   10   23
4. 9   7   16
5. 36   8   28
6. 45   10   5   40

Figure 2.6 *Activity to build an understanding of operations and equality*

Visualizing

To paraphrase Jo Boaler (2016), mathematics is a subject that allows for precise thinking, but it is when that precise thinking is combined with creativity and visualization that the mathematics comes alive. When we don't ask students to think visually, we miss an incredible opportunity to increase students' understanding and to foster critical connections between the left and right hemispheres of the brain.

To visualize is to picture mentally—a process that draws on the right hemisphere of the brain to support the work of the left hemisphere. After many experiences with cubes, tiles, ten-frames and base ten blocks, we need to help students visualize what they might have drawn or constructed without actually drawing or constructing. In the world of fractions, this means that students are gradually able to build a "visualization repertoire" for "three-quarters" that might include three silver quarter coins, pizza, a measuring cup, window panes, or a ruler, each of which serves as a powerful visual representation with which to build fluency with fractions.

What Visualizing Looks Like

Here's what we observed in a third-grade classroom. "We've been using different representations to model our addition and subtraction problems. Now, here is what I would like you to do. For the problem 192 – 55, I want you to visualize how you can represent this problem and then describe what you see to your partner. For this task we won't be using materials or whiteboards or paper. We'll just be picturing mathematics in our heads. Then we will share what we see with the whole class."

Here is some of what the students reported that left us convinced that they were well on their way toward developing strong numerical fluency:

> *I saw a bar model. There was a bar with 192 on the top and a second bar with 55 underneath it. I know that I can add on to the 55 to find the difference.*

> *I pictured a number line with an arrow at 192. I drew an arrow to the left and wrote 55 on the arrow so that I knew I had to count back 55.*

> *I pictured base ten blocks. There was one hundred, nine tens, and two ones, and I pictured myself removing six tens and putting five back.*

> *I visualized money and saw a dollar, nine dimes, and two pennies. In my mind I changed one of the dimes into ten pennies and then I removed five dimes and five pennies.*

Verbalizing or Describing What and How

Verbalizing—or describing what you see or what you are thinking—is a crucial step in the transition from concrete and representational to abstract understanding. Verbalizing gives students the opportunity to hear themselves thinking and to share that thinking (see Figure 2.7). Building on constructions, graphical representations, and their visualizations, verbalizing adds language to the mix, thereby strengthening the connections within the brain among executive processing, visual, language, and memory functions.

Verbalizing serves four main purposes:

1. Verbalizing provides the opportunity to describe mathematical entities. For example, given the number sentence: $(7 \times 3) + 1 = 22$, students should be able to verbalize that "there were seven rows of three and I had one left over, so I had twenty-two."

2. Verbalizing allows children to confirm understanding of operations, first for themselves and then for others. For example, when asked "What is the meaning of $7 + 3 = 10$?" a first grader might verbally explain that the set of seven grew larger: "I had seven marbles and I got three more, so my answer is a bigger number. It is ten."

3. Verbalizing surfaces key vocabulary and asks students to use this vocabulary in their explanations.

4. Verbalizing also enables students and their teachers to focus on language and descriptions of how and what students are thinking. For example, after drawing a bar model to represent an addition problem, students might tell us that "Since the girl had fifteen cookies in all, I drew a rectangle and labeled it 'fifteen.' Then since she ate six cookies, I cut the bar into two pieces and made the smaller piece 'six.'"

Of course students use verbalization to explain their thinking and justify their answers, but we prefer to differentiate these more formal explanations or discussions of "why" from the descriptions of "what" and "how" that must precede justifying.

Figure 2.7 *Verbalizing adds language to the mathematical mix.*

What Verbalization Looks Like

Imagine a first-grade class asked to describe what they notice to their classmates about the arrangement of blocks shown in Figure 2.8. Notice the purpose is to "describe," not yet to "justify."

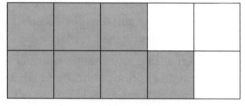

Keisha says: *I see two rows of three and one more.*

Cal says: *I can see three groups of two and one left over. I know there are seven.*

Sam says: *I see a ten-frame showing seven.*

Figure 2.8 *Block arrangement*

Amanda says: *I see some shaded blocks and three unshaded blocks.*

Note how verbalization and describing surface critical vocabulary, like "groups" and "rows" and "more," even in this simple example. Notice too how describing provided a natural lead-in to justifying and reminds us of the power of the simple "What do you notice?" question.

Justifying or Discussing Why

When we value student thinking as something that is just as important as simply getting correct answers, we need to create classroom norms that expect students to justify their work and their thinking. In fact, being able to justify one's answer is often more important than getting the right answer because the justification often reveals misunderstandings and surfaces mistakes. We have found that justifying is easily stimulated by such questions as:

Why do you say that?

Why do you think that?

Can you explain that, please?

Who doesn't agree? Why not?

Who did it differently and can explain how their approach is different?

Convince us that you are right (whether the answer is correct or incorrect).

When we ask students to justify their thinking or to convince the class that what they did or said is correct, we are attending to two critical Common Core Standards for Mathematical Practice: #2, "Reason abstractly and quantitatively";

and #3, "Construct viable arguments and critique the reasoning of others" (National Governors Association 2010). What capability is more important for our students in the future than an ability to construct and critique viable arguments in their writing, their mathematics work, their science learning, throughout social studies, and in life in general?

What Justifying Looks Like

Consider fourth graders talking about how they know that 23 × 7 is 161.

> *I know seven 25s is 175. So, 23 is two less than 25, so I multiplied 2 times 7 and got 14. I subtracted 14 from 175 and got 161.*

> *First, I know that the answer is going to have a 1 in the ones place because 7 times 3 is 21, so I think 161 is right.*

> *I multiply 20 times 7 and get 140 and 7 times 3 and get 21. 140 + 21 is 161.*

This justification can come verbally or in writing, and with visuals. The important point is that to be fluent, one must be able to justify one's answer and support one's justification with words, pictures, and/or symbols.

Putting the Six Processes Together

Consider presenting the table in Figure 2.9 to a class of third graders.

Vegetable or fruit	Number needed	Cost
Tomatoes	5	49¢ each
Cucumbers	3	85¢ each
Lettuce	2	$1.50 per bunch
Green peppers	4	69¢ each
Peaches	8	75¢ each
Apples	7	85¢ each

Figure 2.9 *Food order for salad and dessert*

Presenting and posting a table of data like this is the perfect stimulus for a "what do you notice?" and "what do you wonder?" discussion to build familiarity with a context and stimulate student interest. We hear students, after talking with their partners, announce to the class:

> *I see fruits and vegetables.*
>
> *I see that lettuce is the most expensive.*
>
> *I notice that you need less than ten of each item.*
>
> *We see that you need the most number of peaches.*

Rather than limit this problem to something as narrow as how much the apples cost, teachers who use "What do you wonder?"—a form of contextualizing—get to choose from such student-provided tasks as:

> *Which item do you spend the most money for?*
>
> *Which item do you spend the least money for?*
>
> *About how much does the entire order cost?*
>
> *What does the entire order cost?*

Within the context of this story or situation, and starting with "Which item costs the most?" teachers can lead students to strategize about which items cannot possibly cost the most and why—thereby supporting estimation skills. They can then ask students to focus on the apples and the peaches and ask students to use base ten blocks, a picture, and a number sentence to help them represent the situation—thereby focusing on multiple representations (including constructing, drawing, and visualizing). Teachers can then help students further develop numerical fluency through such questions as:

> *Can you explain how these representations are the same?* (verbalizing)
>
> *How are they different?* (verbalizing)
>
> *Turn and explain to your partner how you know how much the peaches will cost.* (justifying)

The numerical fluency we are seeking is evident in a classroom where students share and explain such insights as:

> *If there were ten peaches, you would pay $7.50. But two fewer peaches would be $1.50 less—so the peaches cost $6.*
>
> *I thought that 75 cents is seven dimes and five pennies. So I'd need 56 dimes and 40 pennies. That's $5.60 plus 40 cents or $6.*

> *I knew that two peaches would cost $1.50, so four would be $3 and eight would have to be $6.*

Note how a table of data provides a context and how our questions provide students with the opportunity to construct, represent, visualize, verbalize, and justify. And this is only one of many problems and tasks our students can wrestle with, based solely on one data table and the notice-wonder launch (see Max Ray-Riek's *Powerful Problem Solving* [2013] for more on this) when the six processes guide our work.

Conclusion

We know what constitutes good instruction. It is evident in classrooms wherever students link mathematics to real situations, represent the situations with objects and/or drawings, describe what they see, and justify their thinking. These are the processes that need to be front and center wherever and whenever mathematics is being taught.

Chapter 3

Classroom Structures for Developing Numerical Fluency

In Chapter 1 we described the pivotal understandings that we believe are necessary for children to attain numerical fluency. In Chapter 2, we defined a set of processes to teach these pivotal ideas. In this chapter, we identify and describe a set of teaching structures that enhance instruction of numerical fluency. For each of these structures we provide a description of the structure and why it can be valuable, some teaching tips for using the structure, and explanations of how the structure supports the development of numerical fluency. Chapters 4 through 9 each include a set of classroom activities that use one or more of these structures.

Guiding Principles for Teaching Structures

There are several guiding principles that apply to these structures and their use in developing numerical fluency:

- Fluency takes time and, when based on conceptual understanding rather than rote memorization, requires the integration of ideas.

- Fluency cannot be developed in a single day, during a single lesson, or with a single speed test.

- There is no "one and done" when teaching numerical fluency. Thinking metaphorically, building numerical fluency is like building a wall—one that will last a lifetime. Each brick requires a pre-assessment of the task, careful placement, glue, adjustment, regluing or glazing, and then time to become a part of the whole wall.

The structures we introduce here are number talks, games, problem-solving activities, word problem banks, and student-constructed materials.

Number Talks

Number talks are powerful structures, not only for developing fluency, but also for using explanation to develop understanding of numbers and operations.

What Are Number Talks?

Sherry Parrish (2010) codified the powerful strategy of number talks with the publication of her book *Number Talks: Helping Children Build Mental Math and Computation Strategies, Grades K–5*. Teachers everywhere have adopted this strategy to build fluency and flexibility with numbers. At its simplest, a number talk presents a numerical problem to students, then gives them some time to mentally find the solution and then to use a signal to note that they have a solution. Teachers collect student answers and students get to present the various ways they arrived at the answer.

A Sample Number Talk

Consider a class of second graders wrestling with 95 – 48 without access to pencil or paper. After a chance to think individually, students then share out approaches like:

> *I counted up from 48 by 2 to get to 50 and knew I have 45 more to go so the answer is 47.*

> *I thought of the 95 as 8 tens and 15 ones and subtracted 4 tens and 8 ones and got 4 tens and 7 ones or 47.*

> *I thought that 95 minus 45 was 50, but you took away 3 more so the answer is 47.*

> *I knew that 48 and 50 was 98, so I needed to go 3 less than 50 which is 47 to get 95.*

For an example of an effective number talk, see the video at **hein.pub/NumericalFluency** (click on Companion Resources)

Done right, number talks are great opportunities to focus on strategies, thinking, and alternative approaches. They also help teachers shift the focus from their teaching to student thinking. Wrong answers are treated with the same respect as right answers and students are given the opportunity to explain how they got their wrong answer. Most often, this results in a wonderful "oooh I made a mistake" comment as the student self-corrects.

Number Strings

Number strings are a sequence of number talks that encourage students to use one result to find another. For example:

$4 \times 7 =$

$4 \times 70 =$

$40 \times 70 =$

$400 \times 700 =$

Number strings are usually constructed to help students move from easy or known understandings to more advanced understandings and to get students to focus on number relationships. The number string above helps develop fluency with multiplying multiples of tens and hundreds based on patterns that emerge from building on 4×7.

Another number string might focus on halving one of the factors, as in:

$3 \times 6 =$

$1\frac{1}{2} \times 6 =$

$\frac{3}{4} \times 6 =$

A number string like this is a powerful way to help students make sense of multiplying by fractions and mixed numbers.

For more ideas about number talks and number strings, we urge you to take a look at www.mathtalks.net or Sherry Parrish's *Number Talks* (2010) or Ruth Parker and Cathy Humphreys' *Making Number Talks Matter* (2015).

How Do Number Talks Support Numerical Fluency?

Number talks often rely on mental math and therefore encourage students to visualize and verbalize relationships between numbers. Very often strategies for making a 10, 100, or 1000 are part of students' thinking. Sometimes strategies like doubles and doubles plus one or multiplying/dividing by ten are also part of the discussion. These provide "teachable moments" when teachers can make use of students' strategies and number sense to reinforce numerical fluency.

In addition, wrong answers often yield greater understanding for both the child who is incorrect as well as those who "got it." For the person who knows the correct answer, there is validation and the opportunity to investigate the incorrect answer; that is, to consider how the other student thought about the problem. For the child with the wrong answer there are lots of opportunities to learn more than just the right answer. One can correct the misconception, adjust a computational error, grasp a new understanding of the concept, or even self-correct. All of these are parts of the process of becoming numerically fluent.

Using Number Talks

Number talks can be conducted at various times during the school day. We have seen teachers use them as an opening part of the math class, a reflection on a piece of homework, or an extended talk during concept development. Some teachers have daily discussions centered around a calendar and choose to take part of that time to incorporate a brief number talk about the day's date. Others use money (such as a classroom coin collection), or a solution for an equation. Some teachers use number talks in place of a drill sheet or speed test, thereby shifting the focus from getting a lot of answers to strategizing and explaining why a few of these answers are correct and make sense.

Games

Students love games that they understand how to play and that offer challenge and fun. Teachers have used games for years to provide opportunities for practice and strategy development.

What Are Math Games and How Do They Support Numerical Fluency?

Math games are one of the most effective forms of practice for developing numerical fluency. Games—whether competitive or just friendly—offer children the opportunity to understand why fluency, strategy, and understanding are important. Games can also allow children to see firsthand how operations work. Playing games provides a real context for students to apply and talk about the math they are learning. The games we are talking about engage children in real mathematical thinking. The more a game relies on problem solving, the more strategy and reasoning are involved with each play.

A special feature for teachers implementing math games in their classrooms is the opportunity to watch children think and to see how they solve problems (see Figure 3.1). One can easily see if a child can make 5 when he or she has a deck containing number cards for 2, 3, 4, and 6. The child who picks up the cards quickly and says "two and three make five" has some fluency to 5. The child who counts on his fingers or takes a long time to solve the problem is not fluent. This offers teachers a window into children's thinking.

An Example: Make a Number

Let's look at the Make a Number game with the challenge of getting closest to 250. Players each draw four cards. The object is to make a number closest to 250 (either greater or less than 250) using three of the four cards and discarding the one remaining card. Once children have made their number, they compare how close they got to 250. The player with the smallest difference wins.

For example, suppose player A draws a 9, 1, 7, 0 and player B draws 6, 7, 8, 2. Player A says "I made 179. I'm tossing my 0 and I'm 71 away from 250." Player B says "I made 276 and I'm tossing my 8 and I'm 26 away from 250. I win this round because my difference from 250 is smaller." Note that player B could have created 267 and been even closer, but would still have won the round. Players engage in five rounds and the player closest to 250 the most times is the winner. This game provides practice with place value, finding differences, reasoning to make the number closest to 250, and choosing a card to discard. It also offers the teacher opportunities to observe how well students estimate, how deeply they understand place value, and how they strategize to find the difference of two numbers.

Figure 3.1 *Math games engage students in both fun and reasoning.*

Using Games

Math is supposed to be challenging, but it is also supposed to be fun. Ideally, math occurs during the day in more than just "math time." The powerful advantage of games is that they provide *both* the challenge *and* the fun as students wrestle, at virtually any time during the day, with accessible tasks that support the development of numerical fluency. We most love it when students extend these activities on their own and/or create new games to challenge their fellow students.

Whether before school, embedded in the school day, after school, or at home, games offer engaging, active learning, and meaningful math practice. Here are some quick tips for successfully implementing math games:

1. Create an understanding that these math games are part of children's work, not just idle play. That is, games should be opportunities to play with a purpose—a chance for students to be learning and practicing mathematics often without even realizing that they are learning. As such, expect them to follow all of your usual classroom expectations and routines.

2. Preview every game with the class or with small groups so that students understand the procedures and rules of the game, how to win, and appropriate math talk during the game. It is best to play a game at least twice—you vs. the class—before allowing independent gaming.

3. Model and encourage an atmosphere of fair play and good sportsmanship.

4. Set clear guidelines for returning the game or the materials to their proper place.

5. Take time to debrief the gaming experience with discussion about what students learned from the game and what strategies they used.

6. Once the mechanics of the game are clear and practiced, expect students to record their results. Recording helps to solidify learning. In some cases, recording is a necessary part of the game.

7. Remind players that many games are based on chance and that everyone will have an opportunity to win, so no sadness for losing is necessary. Games that are based on strategy require many iterations before effective strategies become clear.

Word Problem Banks

Another powerful structure we have seen teachers make very effective use of is the word problem bank.

What Are Word Problem Banks?

In most of the following chapters we have provided banks or collections of word problems meant to offer teachers a resource for ongoing practice. These word problems are opportunities for students to employ the language of operations as well as find sums, differences, products, and quotients in the context of problem situations. Regularly contextualizing the language of operations promotes understanding of those operations, and therefore also develops numerical fluency. Fact practice and computing with larger numbers are natural parts of word problems, but solving these problems is far more productive than completing pages of naked practice problems.

Here is an example of three word problems as they might appear in a bank. Note the opportunity to model these situations, discuss the appropriate operation to be used, create number sentences, and use fact fluency to arrive at and justify solutions.

> Mr. Jones has an apple orchard. Today he picked 4 bags of apples. Each bag has 3 apples. How many apples did he pick?
>
> Mr. Jones picked 24 apples. He put 3 apples in each bag. How many bags would he need?
>
> Mr. Jones picked 18 apples. He had 6 bags. How many apples would be in each bag if each bag contained the same number of apples and all of the apples were packed in bags?

How Do Word Problem Banks Support Numerical Fluency?

Numerical fluency is achieved, in part, by contextualizing mathematical situations such as those represented in these problems. In addition, the problems in problem banks provide practice with the language of mathematical operations, experiences making sense of problems, opportunities to draw pictures and write equations, and practice with writing number sentences. Fact and computational fluency is also embedded in this work. In summary, problem banks offer continual opportunities to develop students' operational sense and their computational fluency.

Using Word Problem Banks

Problem banks are not intended to be used in a single lesson or placed on a single test. Rather, they are places to turn to draw two or three problems once or twice

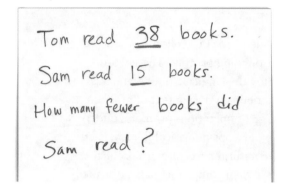

Figure 3.2 *Sharing a problem with students*

a week as part of cumulative review, classwork, or homework.

We often see teachers post one or two problems for students to solve (see Figure 3.2). Individuals, pairs, or groups work to answer the question using varied representations approaches. For example, some students choose to draw a picture of the real objects while others may choose circles or rectangles to represent the problem. Some students may use an algorithm while others might solve the problem mentally. In addition, for all problem bank work students should be expected to create a number sentence that represents the problem, show how they solved the problem, and write the solution in a complete sentence.

Problem-Solving Activities

Just as there are number talks and games, there are also problem-solving activities that teachers can use to support the development of numerical fluency. In this section, we look at several such activities and discuss how best to use them in your classroom.

What Are Problem-Solving Activities?

Problem-solving activities engage curious minds in seeking answers and usually involve a strategy to solve a problem. This involves students in higher-level thinking, greater engagement, and often, greater learning. There is a difference between simple, routine word problems (like those in the problem banks described above) and problem solving as we use it here. Routine word problems like those in problem banks can be answered by applying operational understanding, fact memory, and computational fluency. When completing problem-solving activities, on the other hand, students are encouraged to be curious, find multiple solutions, and look for patterns, thereby raising the level of engagement and learning.

An example of a problem-solving activity might be something as straightforward as the following:

Use the numbers 0, 1, 2, 3, 4, and 5 to find as many different sums as you can. No number can be used more than once. Can you make 1? 2? 3? Can you make every whole number between 1 and 15? Which numbers can you make in the most number of different ways?

There are many possibilities for answers (see Figure 3.3), thus inviting all to participate and giving rise to numerical fluency in an exciting way. Remember that when a child has arrived at a wrong answer, this too makes them think and learn when the errors are questioned.

Use 0, 1, 2, 3, 4, 5 to make as many numbers as you can.	
Make 1	1 + 0
Make 2	1 + 1
Make 3	2 + 1
Make 4	3 + 1
Make 5	4 + 1, 2 + 3
Make 6	5 + 1, 4 + 2, 1 + 2 + 3
Make 7	3 + 4, 5 + 2, 4 + 2 + 1
Make 8	

Figure 3.3 *Making numbers*

How Do Problem-Solving Activities Support Numerical Fluency?

Because problem-solving activities have the potential to so thoroughly engage children in learning, they act as vehicles for developing numerical fluency. Asking students to "find all of the possible ways to make a quarter, using pennies, nickels, and dimes" results in dozens of problems that practice adding using ones, fives, and tens. As they work on problem-solving tasks like this, children get far more dynamic and meaningful fact practice than could ever be achieved with a

20-exercise worksheet or speed test. Equally important, students doing problem-solving activities with a partner often get immediate feedback on mistakes and wrong answers. And best of all, problem-solving activities send the message that solving, thinking, and justifying are far more important than being the first to finish. In short, problem-solving activities involve students in ways that bring joy to mathematics, increase curiosity about relationships, and cannot help but advance numerical fluency.

Using Problem-Solving Activities

Throughout the following chapters, we suggest a wide range of such problem-solving activities. These can be used to engage the whole class or a small group. Teachers can pose the problem, providing the minimum amount of information and direction to activate excitement and engagement of the task at hand, and then send students off to work individually or in groups. Charts on large paper can be used for gallery walks during which students study the work of other groups, and for the development of "class lists" that get added to over time.

As the problem is brought to a close, the teacher reviews what has been discovered. In other cases, a small group may be charged with finding solutions and presenting them. Teachers can open up discussion for further solutions or observations.

Student-Made Materials

Finally, we have seen teachers make effective and creative use of student-made materials to save money and to provide students with a sense of ownership of the materials they use to develop mathematical understanding.

What Are Student-Made Materials and Tasks?

Throughout the following chapters there are also suggestions for students to make and use their own materials. While making these materials and developing tasks, students construct understanding about relationships between and among numbers. They also experience the power of visualization when the materials involve creating representations. For example (see Figure 3.4), when investigating multiplying a number by itself, students can be asked to start with a $1'' \times 1''$ square and then, in teams, to create a set of all the subsequent squares up to $10'' \times 10''$. Students can then be asked: Can you tell the area of each square? Can you predict the areas for 11×11 to 20×20? How? Is there a pattern? What do you notice about areas of odd and even squares?

How Do Student-Made Materials Support Numerical Fluency?

When students create their own materials, they build ownership of these materials. In addition, creating materials fosters both visualization (as they are created) and verbalization (as students follow directions). For example, consider a class of first graders where each student creates his or her own set of 0- to 9-bean sticks by gluing red lima beans onto popsicle sticks, and then uses these bean sticks as personalized, concrete tools to support the learning of one-digit addition and subtraction facts.

Figure 3.4 *1 × 1, 2 × 2, 3 × 3, and 4 × 4 squares*

Using Student-Made Materials

We suggest that the creation of student-made materials be a project for the whole class, so teachers can help students construct them. For example (see Figure 3.5), consider a whole-class activity in which students construct a set of 11 ten-frame cards that show 0 to 10. Students can be told that with each successive card, they should fill in the same number of dots as on the previous card and add one more dot going across until five are filled on the top row. Then proceed down to the left corner of the second row. Continue to fill circles for the card, adding an additional dot on each card.

When students finish constructing their cards, instruct them to lay all eleven cards out in front of them, starting with none or 0 and going to 10. Have children pick up a card such as the 3 card. Then ask, "What do you see?"

Figure 3.5 *Ten-frames*

I see three filled and two unfilled on the top row.

I see two unfilled on the top row and five unfilled on the bottom row.

I see three filled and seven unfilled.

After visualizing and verbalizing each of the eleven cards, pair children together to practice their cards. Change pairs frequently so children get to hear each other speak about the relationships and what they've visualized. When you are sure children can talk about their cards, send them home with a letter for practice.

This is just one example of student-made materials whose construction takes precious classroom time but whose benefits far outweigh the time spent. There are obviously occasions when purchased materials like base ten blocks or linking cubes are appropriate. However, when students create materials like bean sticks or number cards or their own ten-frames, they are empowered with easily accessible tools for use in school and at home to support their learning.

Conclusion

Throughout this book you will find references to each of these five structures as you encounter different suggestions for implementing numerical fluency in your classroom. We strongly advocate that these structures of number talks, games, problem-solving activities, word problem banks, and student-made materials be used as replacements for the mindless drill and practice worksheets that have dominated so many experiences in math class, with very spotty success.

PART TWO

Developing Addition and Subtraction Fluency

Chapter 4

It All Begins with Parts and Wholes

As we said when discussing the pivotal understandings in Chapter 1, understanding what the whole is, what the parts are, how they are related, and what might be missing in a particular problem are all critical aspects of numerical fluency. While parts and wholes are particularly important foundational ideas in kindergarten and first grade for introducing addition and subtraction, these ideas reappear and are just as important in multiplication, division, and fractions. These ideas are not obvious to young children and emerge gradually from experiences with numbers and operations that employ each of the six processes presented in Chapter 2.

In this chapter, we discuss why parts and wholes matter so much, present several key ideas and skills students need to grasp and master, describe a set of classroom activities that support the learning of these skills and ideas, and close with a model sequence of lessons that pulls all of these ideas together.

Why Parts and Wholes Matter

Before more formal learning about the operations of addition and subtraction and the use of symbols, children must recognize that all quantities are comprised of parts and wholes. A well-developed understanding of parts and wholes is the conceptual underpinning of all addition, subtraction, multiplication, and division, and the development of numerical fluency.

The foundational understanding that develops over time as a result of an ongoing stream of learning experiences is that a quantity of objects represented by a numeral (5) and a number word (five) can be broken up into smaller sets, sometimes called subsets. Parts and wholes arise from the physical acts of joining two or more sets of objects to form a whole and separating a whole into two or more parts. These reciprocal actions of putting together and taking apart, when accompanied by numbers and language, are the foundation for all mathematical operations. Sometimes the parts are equal and sometimes they are not. Sometimes the parts and wholes are addends and sums related by addition, and sometimes they are factors and products related by multiplication. And eventually the parts are fractions of the whole.

Key Ideas and Skills

To build fluency with parts and wholes, students need to master three key ideas and their related skills: recognizing small wholes instantly (subitizing), understanding and using +1 and −1, and composing and decomposing numbers.

Subitizing and Seeing Small Wholes

Doug Clements (1999, 405) defines *subitizing* as "the direct perceptual apprehension of the numerosity of a group, or more informally, 'instantly seeing how many.'" It is important for students to be able to visualize small numbers in different configurations, and to recognize those small sets within larger sets. People can learn to recognize sets of up to about five instantly; larger groups can't be subitized, but we learn to recognize the smaller sets within those groups and combine them almost instantly. For example, we want students to be able to see three buttons instantly, and then to recognize six buttons as two groups of three, four and two, or five and one. With repeated practice, children can come to see that all numbers from six to ten are made of the smaller sets they can recognize. This ability to see small wholes and how they can be combined is fundamental to fluency.

Look at what happens when students are asked how many dots there are in the configuration in Figure 4.1, and how they saw them. Not only are these students subitizing, they are also developing a strong sense of parts and wholes.

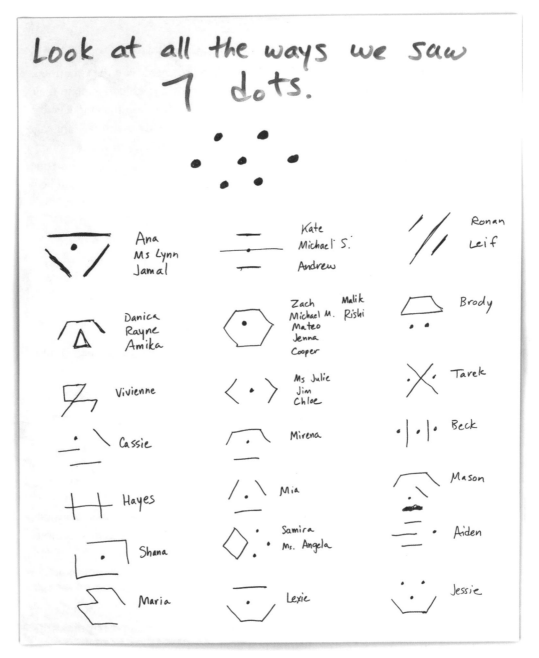

Figure 4.1 *Ways of seeing seven dots*

Knowing Plus 1 and Minus 1

Often we ask, "What is one more than two?" We hear many children respond with "one more than two is three"; however, when presented with the equation 2 + 1, they resort to using fingers to find the answer and are unable to explain their thinking. This is because they do not have a connection between the language of "one more than" and the +1 number sentence. The same is true with the language of "What number is next?" or "What number comes after?" When we are counting on, we are in fact adding one, just as when we count back we are subtracting one. This understanding that *one more than* and *the number that comes next* can be represented as +1 is critical. This is equally true for the relationship between *one less than* and *what number comes before*, with −1.

Moreover, the "plus one facts" also arise and play a critical role in other numerical fluency strategies. The "doubles plus one" and "doubles minus one" facts (such as thinking of 4 + 5 as "double 4 plus one" or "double 5 minus one" help students build on doubles facts—often among the easiest for students to remember—and gives them another tool to build fluency. We can also use "plus one" when we add nines. Because 9 + 1 is 10 (see Pivotal Understanding 6 in Chapter 1), when adding 3 and 9, some children decompose the 3 into 2 + 1 and add 2 to 10 to get 12. Other children add 10 to 3 (based on understanding that 10 is one more than 9), get 13, and then take the added 1 away from 13 to get 12.

Composing and Decomposing Numbers

As we introduced in Chapter 1, composing and decomposing numbers and under-standing what the whole and parts are, how they are related, and what is missing, are all critical aspects of numerical fluency. These ideas are not obvious to young children and emerge gradually from experience with numbers and operations.

One way to emphasize these relationships, common in the Singapore curriculum, is the number bond (shown in Figure 4.2). The whole goes in the top circle, and the parts are written in the circles below.

Of course these are not magic and do not instantly teach children to know the relationships, but they are very helpful in a number of ways.

First, it is helpful for children to see the many different number bonds that can be derived from one number, as shown in Figure 4.3.

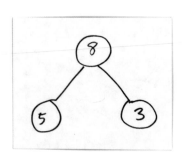

Figure 4.2 *Number bond*

Second, number bonds can help children recombine parts of numbers to make familiar sums. In the problem 7 + 5, if the child uses a number bond to see that 7 is 5 + 2, then it is easier to add the two fives and then the two, using a "make a ten" strategy (5 + 5 + 2 = 10 + 2 = 12). Third, if used correctly, number bonds provide wonderful contextual practice with the language of wholes and parts, and with helping students make sense of problem situations. Students can draw a number bond to determine what is being asked for in a problem.

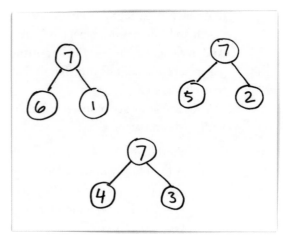

Figure 4.3 *Number bonds for 7*

Consider the problem, "Sarah has 10 orange and yellow super balls. 3 are yellow. How many are orange?" Drawing a number bond here can help the child discern what they have—The whole? A part? What? We see that Sarah has 10 balls and the rest of the story talks about part of them, so 10 is the whole and goes at the top of the bond. We know that 3 balls are yellow and the rest are orange, so 3 is a part and goes in one part of the bond. The other part is still unknown, so that must be what we are looking for. This graphic organizer helps demystify the problem.

Finally, it is important to remember number bonds are not simply "flash cards" for drilling fluency. Rather, they are powerful tools for helping students make the most sense out of the whole and the parts, and to find, for instance, the elusive missing addend as in the problem above. Number bonds help students build the fluency in composing and decomposing numbers that they will need.

■ Classroom Activities

We maximize learning when our students are consistently contextualizing, constructing, representing, verbalizing, visualizing, and justifying, and the following activities reflect these processes. More specifically, the foundation of numerical fluency is clear and unquestioning understanding that, for instance, a group of one and a group of three combine or are joined to create a group of four; and that two parts (or more) become a whole or a total. It is critical that early instruction uses objects (constructing), pictures (representing), and descriptive words (verbalizing) to develop these ideas. Contextualizing, such as using statements like "Brad had 1 pencil and found 3 more pencils," grounds the conceptual work in real situations. And in each case there is the opportunity to ask "How do you know it is 4?" which generates explanations (justifying) that include counting, counting on, converting to 2 plus 2, etc.

We encourage two different kinds of activities to support numerical fluency with parts and wholes:

- short, daily number activities that encourage the building of mental agility with numbers and a good sense of number relationships; and

- more intensive story-telling activities with modeling that encourage the growth of understanding of the meaning of operations.

In the following sections, we take a look at some activities in both of these categories that address the key ideas and skills discussed above.

Daily Number Activities

See It—Say It

One game to practice subitizing is See It—Say It. This is a simple opportunity first to help students recognize small quantities and then to link them to their number names and, eventually, numerals.

Have children close their eyes. Display three counters where they can be seen by all of the children (using an electronic whiteboard, magnetic counters, or whatever you have). Tell the children to open their eyes and let them see the counters for no more than five seconds. Then cover the display and ask the children, "How many did you see?" We have observed kindergarten and first-grade teachers build suspense and excitement by saying: "Ready? Open your eyes and see it." After silent viewing of the display for a few seconds, teachers say: "Time's up. Now say what you saw." It's reasonably easy to get a sense of who saw the quantity correctly and who didn't. Then show the display again and count the objects to reinforce the correct quantity.

We encourage teachers to do this over and over with numbers 1–5 in different arrangements. This can also be done with individual students or small groups using dot cards or other representations. As students move from counting and subitizing to numerals, it is easy to provide students with a set of numeral cards with 1, 2, 3, 4, and 5. Instead of See It—Say It, the game shifts to See It—Say It—Show It.

We find that this "see it—say it—show it" approach makes for perfect quick, daily number investigations. Moreover, this activity is easily expanded from small numbers represented with dot cards to larger numbers represented with number blocks or bean sticks or in expanded notation as students progress through the grades.

Finding Quantities in the Environment

Engage children in a discussion about finding quantities in the classroom by asking such questions as:

> *I am looking for some things in the classroom. Can you help me find two of something?*
>
> *What did you find? Can anyone else find another group of two of something?*
>
> *Can you find three of something the same? How did you find it? What is it? How are you sure it is actually three?*
>
> *Does anyone see one more than three of something? We found two green crayons, how many more do we need to have five?*
>
> *Can you help me find five of something?*

You can extend these questions to the playground ("Can anyone see three people playing together or four children on the swings?"); or to a walk around school ("Can you find two of something? Tires on the sidewalk side of the car?" etc.).

Also, these activities are great homework for kindergarten and early first grade. Send home a sheet that says, "Find things at home that you found two of (or three, four, five, etc.). Use words, numerals, or pictures to show us what you found." To enrich this activity, you might want to ask children to find things that are one less than six or two more than three. Again, this is good practice with language and the next level of experience in adding to or taking apart from the original set.

"Show Me" Finger Play

Finger play helps to solidify students' understanding of five (see Pivotal Understanding 5 in Chapter 1), and it encourages young children to see small quantities quickly and associate them with their numerical names.

To begin this game, it is helpful to have children sit in a circle where they can see each other. Begin by having children put both hands behind their back. Ask them to use one hand to show you a quantity. Watch closely to see the children who can quickly show you the quantity and those who have to count their fingers.

Start by modeling and saying, "I am going to put my hands behind my back. When I say 'Show me one finger,' put your hand up with one finger. When I say 'two,' show me two fingers. Are you ready? Let's go. Show me one!" (Show one finger on one hand, then put your hand back behind your back.) Repeat with "Show me two," "Show me three," etc., up to five. Then repeat the process with the numbers out of sequence.

Another version of this is to use two hands to show a total quantity. In this exercise, children see parts and wholes and realize that small numbers are in big numbers.

Tell students, "Now use one or both hands to make the number I ask you to show me."

"Show me three." Jess held up two fingers on one hand and one on another. Jacob held up three fingers on one hand.

"Show me four." Stephan held up four fingers on one hand and made a fist with the other to indicate zero.

In both of these cases, this activity is a great opportunity to see which children are showing their fingers with automaticity, and which ones are still relying on counting. You could also repeat the activity using five counters rather than fingers. But importantly, this activity opens great opportunities to discuss different "arrangements" of the same number, as in why Jess and Jacob used different fingers to represent the same number.

After many practices with the two versions above and for those who show the quantity with ease, try these extensions. Ask, "Now can you show me one more than three? How many are you showing now? Can you show me one less than four? How many are you showing?"

Storytelling and Modeling Activities

Number Strips

Inch-wide paper strips constructed with four and five sections can help children visualize and verbalize the parts of four and five. They work well when combined with connecting cubes; students can use the cubes to model different combinations and then color strips to match (see Figure 4.4).

Here is a game using number strips that can reinforce these ideas. Each student in a group of three has five blank five-section strips. Each child takes a turn rolling a 0–5 cube and coloring the matching number of sections on one strip blue (so if the child rolls a 3, they color three sections in one strip blue). Continue until each of the five strips has been used once. Then, the children take turns rolling the cube again. This time, they use another color (e.g., red), and can only color in the result if they have a strip where the quantity fits. So, for example, if a child has a

Figure 4.4
Visualizing parts of four

strip with three sections colored blue and rolls a 2, they can color in the remaining sections of that strip red. But if they roll a 3, they can't color that strip. The first person to color all five strips wins. The winner then tells what each strip shows (e.g., "This strip has five with three blue and two red.").

Storytelling and Acting Out

Practicing storytelling and acting out situations builds comfort for children in solving problems, the language of math, and numerical fluency. Once daily or a few times a week provides ongoing practice with both fluency and operational sense by sharing stories. Over time, students should be expected to create and share their own stories for the class to act out.

Give students a story, or a contextualized problem (see examples below). Encourage students to use manipulatives to move pieces around and make sense of the problem. (Once you have introduced number sentences, encourage students to add them to describe the situation as well.) In class discussions, have students share their reasoning for their solutions. Use questions like the following to encourage justification:

> *How did you get your answer?*
>
> *Can you show us using counters?*
>
> *Did anyone else do this problem a different way?*

Here is a bank of story problems to start you off and to launch students in creating their own story problems. Adjust the nouns and names to your needs.

There are 5 ducks in the pond. 4 ducks are on the outside of the pond. How many ducks are there?

There are 2 big giraffes and 3 baby giraffes. How many giraffes are there?

6 chimps are playing with 3 gorillas. How many animals are there?

Sarah has 3 red flowers and 4 purple flowers. How many flowers are there?

There were 4 boys in line and 5 more came along. How many boys were there?

Max has 3 apple slices on his plate. His mom puts 5 on. How many apple slices does he have?

There were 9 mosquitoes in the back yard. 3 were killed with bug spray. How many mosquitoes are there now?

Sheila starts on 6 and jumps 3 squares. Where does she land?

There are 7 animals. 4 are pigs. How many are not?

There are 4 children. 2 are girls. How many are boys?

Greg and David have 8 apples. David has 6 apples. How many does Greg have?

There are 10 donuts in the box. 6 are plain. How many are not plain?

7 dogs are sleeping. 3 wake up. How many are still sleeping?

We had 9 balloons and 3 popped. How many are left?

Patsy buys 7 small and large lemons. 3 are small. How many are large?

I see 6 crabs on the shore. 2 crawl away. How many are still in the sand?

Sam has 9 toys. 4 are cars and the rest are planes. How many are planes?

There are 10 eggs in the basket and 3 break. How many are left?

Alicia blows 8 soap bubbles. They all pop. How many are left?

Edgar buys 3 lights on Monday and 5 on Tuesday. How many did he buy?

There are 6 sharks and 2 whales. How many animals are in the water?

Sabra lights 5 candles and blows out 3. How many are still burning?

Devon has 10 buttons that are black and white. 5 are black. How many are white?

David lost 3 balloons and 6 were left. How many did he have before some were lost?

8 children got off the swings. 2 are still on the swings. How many children were on the swings?

Putting It All Together

See, Say, Convince!

Here is a longer-term problem-solving project that enhances visualization and involves using anywhere from two to eight one-inch colored tiles on a three by three grid. Students use the grids to create as many different arrangements of a given number of tiles as they can. We call this See, Say, Convince! It is designed to develop fluency with recognition of quantity and number and to provide an opportunity for problem solving in a concrete and pictorial environment.

Project Rules

Make an arrangement on a three by three grid by coloring in a given number of squares so that at least one side is touching another side. No solely diagonal connections are allowed. You can begin with two squares and go to eight. Figure 4.5, which we first saw in Chapter 1, is an example of students coloring six squares.

Figure 4.5 *Arrangements of six*

Project Materials

> *Three by three squares of one-inch-square grid paper (one per child to start and one for the teacher)*
>
> *One-inch tiles (up to nine for each child)*
>
> *Pencil for each child*
>
> *Markers or crayons for each child*
>
> *Small piece of colored string or yarn*

Implementing the Project in Kindergarten and Grade 1

Figure 4.6 is a schedule for using See, Say, Convince! as a three-week project in kindergarten.

Day 1	Day 2	Day 3	Day 4	Day 5
Introduce.	Practice with 2.	Introduce 3.	Make and color numerous arrangements for 3.	Make and color numerous arrangements for 3.
Day 6	**Day 7**	**Day 8**	**Day 9**	**Day 10**
Play "Say it Fast" with 2 and 3.	Introduce 4.	Make and color numerous arrangements for 4.	Verbalize what they visualize; play "Say it Fast" with 2, 3, 4.	Introduce 5.
Day 11	**Day 12**	**Day 13**	**Day 14**	**Day 15**
Make and color numerous arrangements for 5.	Verbalize what they visualize; play "Say it Fast" with 2, 3, 4, 5.	Introduce 6.	Make and color numerous arrangements for 6.	Verbalize what they visualize; play "Say it Fast" with 2, 3, 4, 5.

Figure 4.6 *See, Say, Convince! schedule*

Day 1

Format: Circle on the floor

Tell students, *Today I have a problem. I have this paper and two one-inch tiles. I have to put these tiles on this paper so that two sides always touch or are next to each other. The tiles cannot connect across from each other or diagonally. So let me show you.* Put down two tiles, one each on A and B.

A	B	C
D	E	F
G	H	I

Now, let's see if this matches our rules. Are the tiles in touching squares? (Yes.)

Are the squares diagonal? (No.)

Good. Then do we have an arrangement of two that meets our rules? (Yes.)

Now let's try this one. (Put tiles on A and D.)

Let's see if that works.

What do I need to check? Who remembers?

The squares are next to each other and not diagonal.

Good. Let's try one more. (Put tiles on A and E.)

Does this work? Does it meet our rules?

Why or why not?

Are the squares sharing a side? NO! They are diagonal!

Use a piece of colored yarn to show a diagonal.

Now does anyone else want to suggest a way to arrange the two tiles so that they fit our rule?

Take at least five suggestions. With every suggestion, ask the class if the new configuration meets the rules.

Day 2

Format: Circle on the floor

Show students two tiles and a blank grid. Ask, *Can anyone tell me what we did yesterday with these two tiles and this paper?* Answers should include: made designs or pictures; used two tiles; had to have sides touch; can't be diagonal.

Ok, today let's color in some of the designs we made yesterday. I think I made this design yesterday (AB). *Is that right? Does it keep to the rules?* (You need to keep asking this question for two reasons: to make sure that everyone understands *next to* and *diagonal* and can say and use the language. Also, as designs get more complex, diagonals will play a bigger role.)

Now I will color in these two squares. To keep track of my coloring, I will mark each square before I color.

Lift each tile and mark the square beneath it.

Did I mark the exact squares where my tiles were?

Color in the squares.

Is my design complete?

Does it look exactly the same?

Do the rules still work?

Here is another one I made yesterday. (AD) Is that right? Does it keep to the rules?

Now I will mark and color in these two squares.

Mark the squares and then color them in.

Did I mark the exact squares where my tile was?

Did I make a picture of my design?

Does it look exactly the same?

Do the rules still work?

Now use your tiles to make a design of two that follows the rules. Try to make your design different from mine.

After students have completed their tile designs, pick five different arrangements and ask students to color them. If you find a duplicate, ask the class if you already have that one and how they know.

Day 3

Format: Class discussion on the rug with the set of designs created the day before.

Let me show you the designs we made yesterday. As I hold them up, tell me fast how many colored squares you see. Flash all the colored squares.

Great job. Today we are going to make an arrangement with three. Here is mine (show ABC). Does it work with the rules? How about this one? (ADG) How about this one? (DEF) And this one? (DEI)

Today, we are going to give you a turn to make designs at your table. You will each have three tiles and a three by three grid.

You will create the design according to our picture.

You need to make sure the design meets our rules.

When you are sure, raise your hand.

I will come and check your work and you will mark your design for coloring.

If I cannot get to you, try to make more designs.

Who can help me go back over these instructions?

Every child goes to their seat and creates a three-square arrangement using tiles and places it on the grid as you move around the room to verify their arrangements. Have them lift the tiles to mark the squares, and then color the arrangement in. Help them copy their design accurately if needed. Keep the designs for the next session.

Days 4–5

Format: Circle on the floor

Let's see what we have here. (Hold up an arrangement of three.)

How many do you see?

How do you know?

Note: At this point you may begin to hear some students counting or talking about seeing two squares and one square. Others may be subitizing, which is the goal for all students.

Does this arrangement fit the rule?

If you only have a few minutes, do as many as you can but do them well and continue the next day until you have done them all.

Day 6

Format: Circle on the floor

For this activity, you will need all the cards the class has made with two and three squares.

Today, I am going to hold up all of the cards we made. All I want you to say is how many colored squares you see.

Here is how we will do it. I will hold up a card. (Show a card with two squares colored in.)

I will say "See" and you will look without calling out.

Then I will say "Say" and you will say the number. It will be fast!

Wait for a silent count of three between "See" and "Say."

Additional Ideas for Grades 1–2

Here are some additional ideas you can use to extend this project in grades 1–2, along with using more tiles.

Telling Stories and Writing Equations

After students have created a range of different arrangements of their colored squares and identified the number of colored squares they see, it is time to model stories about what is shown on the card, ask students to create their own stories, and to write the accompanying number sentence on the back of the card. For example, for a card with three squares filled in, students might suggest that a muffin container has nine places, but only three are filled. How many muffins can be added? On the back, students might write either $9 - 3 = 6$, or $3 + 6 = 9$, or both.

Problem-Solving Challenge

Have we made all the arrangements we can with two? Let's try to make sure we have. How can we do that?

Allow children to explore the arrangements you have by posting them with a magnet on the board or on a poster with tape. Do not arrange them in any order, as that is one of the critical thinking ideas you want them to construct. Facilitate a discussion about which arrangements are missing, which are duplicates, and how we can know that we have made *all* of the possible arrangements. After all of the work that students have done so far, this is where students should be expected to provide arguments or justifications for which arrangements are missing and which are duplicates. We encourage you to ask your students to "convince us that what you propose is true."

For the remaining days, continue with similar activities for four, five, and six squares, first having students create arrangements, and then using the Say It Fast activity.

See Figure 4.7 for a schedule that might be used to adapt these activities to a three-week project for later grade 1 or grade 2.

Day 1	Day 2	Day 3	Day 4	Day 5
Make arrangements for 2 and 3 using tiles and then coloring in to introduce the process of making arrangements of a given number.	Review arrangements of 2 and 3 using tiles and introduce using markers or crayons to create different arrangements of two colored squares.	Talk about and create arrangements of three colored squares in the three by three grid.	Practice with the 2s, including telling stories to go with each and writing equations on the back of the grid.	Practice with the 3s, including telling stories to go with each and writing equations on the back of the grid.
Day 6	Day 7	Day 8	Day 9	Day 10
Say It Fast to recognize arrangements with 2 and 3.	Talk about arrangements of two colors for 5, tell stories to go with each, and write equations on the back of the grid.	Introduce arrangements for 6.	Talk about arrangements of two colors for 6 and tell stories to go with each.	Talk about arrangements of two colors for 6, tell stories to go with each, and write equations on the back of the grid.
Day 11	Day 12	Day 13	Day 14	Day 15
Introduce arrangements for 7.	Talk about arrangements of two colors for 7 and tell stories to go with each.	Talk about arrangements of two colors for 7, tell stories to go with each, and write equations on the back of the grid.	Color 8 all the different ways. Tell stories to go with each and write equations on the back of the grid.	Use posters of all the work that students have done to conduct a gallery walk, and discuss what students learned from this activity.

Figure 4.7 *A schedule for a three-week project in grades 1 or 2*

＊＊＊＊＊

While these ideas of joining and separating parts are elementary to adults and older children, they are the initial building blocks to numerical fluency, and it is worth spending significant time on them in the early grades.

Chapter 5

Developing Fluency with Addition and Subtraction Facts

Here is part of a discussion we overheard in a third-grade class at the beginning of the year when students were asked: "What is 8 + 6 and how do you know?"

> *Well, I know it is 6 + (6 + 2) or double six and add two.*

> *That is not how I did it. I took two off of the six and added it to eight and then I got ten and added four more so fourteen.*

> *I like fives. I know five and three is eight, and five and one is six, so I just added the fives and got ten and added the three and the one to get fourteen.*

> *I decomposed the six into two and four. Then I added eight and two which is ten and added the four that was left to get fourteen.*

> *I didn't do it that way, I counted by twos from eight three times: ten, twelve, fourteen.*

> *Not me. I know that eight plus eight and two less is fourteen.*

This discussion highlights the major messages of this chapter about supporting the development of fluency with addition and subtraction facts. Among these messages are that students use a range of strategies for quickly and efficiently finding these facts, and that the processes of contextualizing, visualizing, and verbalizing are key elements of instruction. In addition, what becomes evident in just this small set of student strategies is the key understanding of getting to ten and going beyond in addition and subtraction—a strategy used by two of these students.

It has been our experience, and that of many elementary teachers, that there is often a serious breakdown when addition and subtraction move above ten. That is, 5 + 4 seems to come much more naturally—perhaps by looking at the fingers on our hands—than 5 + 6, which takes us beyond ten, beyond our fingers, and requires an understanding that eleven represents one 10 and one 1. All of which argues that teaching the "harder" addition and subtraction facts requires careful thought, deeper understanding of strategies and the connections between facts, and a much broader range of activities than timed fluency drills.

In kindergarten, young children are exposed to the notion of grouping tens and ones when studying "teen numbers" as a group of ten and some leftovers. This is followed in first grade by similar investigations of "teen numbers," but this time with one 10 as a unit and some ones. Deep conceptual understanding of teen numbers is essential to mastering addition over ten. It is important to note that our language is highly confusing here as we say the number before the "teen," tricking the brain to write the number first. So thirteen often becomes thirty-one. Understanding that a teen number can be written in expanded notation or 10 +___ will help students become more fluent.

In Chapter 4 we focused on small numbers, contextualizing and visualizing them; now we will take that information and apply it to the addition and subtraction facts to 20. We will move on to even larger numbers in the next chapter.

Key Ideas and Skills

We highlight four key skills and ideas that support the development of fluency with addition and subtraction facts:

- the importance of building from facts to 5, to facts to 10, to facts to 20;
- the need to focus on visualizing and verbalizing;
- the power of doubles, doubles plus and minus one, and doubles plus and minus two; and

■ the need to help students identify which facts they know, which facts they can easily derive from those they already know, and which facts they are not yet secure with and for which they need to develop effective strategies.

Facts to 5, then to 10, and finally to 20

Like so much of mathematics, the mastery of addition and subtraction facts needs to be developed coherently, building fluency with "harder" facts on a strong foundation of "easier" facts.

Whether learning sums of five, adding onto five, repeatedly adding five or rounding up or down from five, understanding the role of five (and then ten) on numerical fluency is very important. Once students have a solid understanding of addition and subtraction to five, they are ready to focus on "five plus" numbers (5 + 1, 5 + 2, etc.) and repeatedly adding 5s to build fluency with facts to 10. Then, upon this foundation of facts to 10, students are well positioned to develop fluency with all addition and subtraction facts.

A lack of fluency with small numbers results in using fingers. *While there is nothing wrong with using fingers—our most accessible manipulative—to support early development of facts, fingers become less and less convenient as we turn to larger facts.* Without deep fluency in small numbers, counting becomes a natural but inefficient strategy. For example, someone who has to count on to find 8 + 5 may never see the relationships of 8, 5, and 13, so that other facts, such as subtracting 13 − 8 = 5, become entirely new problems instead of relationships between numbers. Over time, finger counting to "add on" or "take from" is habit forming and ineffective and too often yields incorrect answers. Adding over ten involves large quantities to hold in the brain and to see in the mind's eye. For these reasons, some sort of strategy is needed to help children add over ten, relying on reasoning rather than finger counting.

Visualizing and Verbalizing

Visuals like dominoes, dot cards, number lines, and ten- and double ten-grids or frames help children visualize and verbalize their strategies as they add and subtract with 10 and then within 20. Figure 5.1 links the processes of contextualizing, visualizing (using the grids) and verbalizing facts to 10, and the classroom questions and language that support student learning. We note that there are various ways to fill ten-grids. In this example, we filled from top to bottom and from left to right to emphasize 5. It is important to note that the "negative" or unfilled spaces are as valuable in visualizing and verbalizing as the filled spaces. This provides practice with "How many more to make ten?"

Contextualizing	Visualizing	Verbalizing
1 child at the market, 9 more come along. How many in all? 9 kids on the playground, and 1 more comes. How many kids? 10 fish in the pond, 9 swim away. How many are left? I had some cookies. I ate 9, now I only have 1. How many did I have to start?		How many filled on the top row? One How many unfilled on the top row? Four Say what you see: four and one is five or $4 + 1 = 5$. How many unfilled on the second row? Five How many unfilled all together? Four on the top row, five on the bottom row, nine unfilled in all. In the whole grid, how many boxes are filled? One In the whole grid, how many are unfilled? Nine Let's say what we see: one filled and nine unfilled make ten in all. $9 + 1 = 10$
2 children at the park and 8 more come. How many children at the park now? 10 cookies were on the plate. 8 are left. How many got eaten? I had 10 pennies. I spent some. I had 8 left. How many did I spend?		How many filled on the top row? Two How many unfilled on the top row? Three Say what you see: two and three make five or $2 + 3 = 5$. How many unfilled on the second row? Five How many unfilled all together? Three on the top row, five on the bottom row, eight unfilled in all. In the whole grid, how many boxes are filled? Two In the whole grid, how many are unfilled? Eight Let's say what we see: two filled and eight unfilled make ten in all. $8 + 2 = 10$

Figure 5.1 *Contextualizing, visualizing, and verbalizing*

Contextualizing	Visualizing	Verbalizing
3 boys were at the game and 7 more came. How many boys? 10 pennies in my pocket. I spent 3. How many left? Some Legos in the basket. I got 3 more. Now I have 10. How many did I get?		How many filled on the top row? Three How many unfilled on the top row? Two Say it: Three and two make five. How many unfilled on the second row? Five How many unfilled all together? Two on the top row, five on the bottom row, seven unfilled in all. In the whole grid, how many boxes are filled? Three How many are unfilled? Seven Let's say what we see: three filled and seven unfilled make ten in all. $3 + 7 = 10$
4 people were in line. 6 more got in line. How many people are in line? I had 10 balloons. 4 popped. How many left? Sarah read 4 books. She has 10 books to read all together. How many books does she have left to read?		How many filled on the top row? Four How many unfilled on the top row? One Say what we see: four and one make five. $4 + 1 = 5$ How many unfilled on the second row? Five How many unfilled all together? One on the top row, five on the bottom row, six unfilled in all. In the whole grid, how many boxes are filled? Four In the whole grid, how many are unfilled? Six Let's say what we see: four filled and six unfilled make ten in all. $4 + 6 = 10$

Figure 5.1 *Contextualizing, visualizing, and verbalizing* (continued)

Contextualizing	Visualizing	Verbalizing
5 friends at the party. 5 more came. How many friends? 10 canned drinks. 5 are open. How many are closed?		How many filled on the top row? Five How many unfilled on the top row? Zero How many unfilled on the second row? Five In the whole grid, how many boxes are filled? Five In the whole grid, how many are unfilled? Five Let's say what we see: five filled and five unfilled make ten in all. $5 + 5 = 10$
6 people waiting to get on the bus. 4 more came along. How many people are waiting to getting on the bus? I had some pennies. I needed 10 to make a dime. Mom gave me 6 and now I have 10. How many did I have to start?		How many filled on the top row? Five How many filled on the second row? One In the whole grid, how many boxes are filled? Six In the whole grid, how many are unfilled? Four Let's say what we see: six filled and four unfilled make ten in all. $6 + 4 = 10$

Figure 5.1 *Contextualizing, visualizing, and verbalizing* (continued)

Contextualizing	Visualizing	Verbalizing
8 chairs at the table. I pulled up 2 more. How many chairs are at the table now? 10 people needed to fill the ride at the amusement park. 8 people are there. How many more people do they need?		How many filled on the top row? Five How many filled on the second row? Three Let's say what we see: five filled on the top, three filled on the bottom, eight filled altogether. $5 + 3 = 8$ In the whole grid, how many are unfilled? Two Let's say what we see: eight filled and two unfilled make ten in all. $8 + 2 = 10$
4 children sitting on the bench and 5 more came. How many kids on the bench? 10 beads needed for a necklace, 9 are on. How many more to be added to complete the necklace?		How many filled on the top row? Five How many filled on the second row? Four Let's say what we see: five filled on the top, four filled on the bottom, nine filled altogether. $5 + 4 = 9$ In the whole grid, how many are unfilled? One Let's say what we see: nine filled and one unfilled make ten in all. $9 + 1 = 10$

Figure 5.1 *Contextualizing, visualizing, and verbalizing* (continued)

Doubles, Doubles Plus and Minus One, Doubles Plus and Minus Two

For many children, "doubling" is just another vocabulary word or rule to add to the list, not a strategy to enhance numeracy. Students fail to comprehend that doubling refers to using the same addend twice, therefore their repertoire of strategies does not include "doubles" and "doubles plus one," two of the easiest strategies of all. It is important to realize that "doubles" and "doubles plus one" are names for powerful strategies which, for children to fully understand them, must be developed with contextualizing, building, visualizing, verbalizing, representing, and justifying.

As an introduction to the language of doubles, play Simon Says:

Simon says build five. Simon says double it. What do you have? 5 + 5 or 10

Simon says build six. Simon says double it. What do you have? 6 + 6 or 12

As modeled in Figure 5.2, filling ten-grids for doubles provides for variations in visualizations and verbalizing and is helpful to a growing number sense. For each of these examples, the justification questions "How do you know that?" "Can you explain your thinking?" and "Can you convince us?" are critical.

Contextualize	Build and visualize	Verbalize	Represent
1 girl in the front seat of the car, 1 in the back seat. 1 and 1 is 2.	Build the first number on the top row and double it by building it again in the second row.	Double: one and one is two.	$1 + 1 = 2$ $2 - 1 = 1$
2 girls in the front and 1 in the back. 3 girls in the swimming pool and 1 gets out. How many are still in the pool?	Add one to make a double plus one.	Double plus one: one and one is two and one more is three.	$(1 + 1) = 2 + 1 = 3$ $3 - 1 = 2$
1 canoe with 2 boys. Another canoe with 2 boys. 2 and 2 is 4. 4 canoers and 2 get out. How many canoers are there now?	Build the first number on the top row and double it by building it again in the second row.	Double: two and two is four.	$2 + 2 = 4$ $4 - 2 = 2$
2 canoes with 2 boys and 1 kayak with 1 boy. 2 and 2 is 4 and 1 more is 5. 5 boys in canoes. 1 canoe turns over. How many boys are now in canoes?	Add one to make a double plus one.	Double plus one: two and two is four and one more is five.	$(2 + 2) + 1 = 5$ $5 - 2 = 3$

Figure 5.2 *Building and verbalizing* (continues)

Contextualize	Build and visualize	Verbalize	Represent
2 triangles next to each other in a drawing. How many line segments? 1 triangle is erased. How many line segments?	Build the first number on the top row and double it by building it again in the second row. (Notice the negative space makes this ten-grid also say $6 + 4 = 10$.)	Double: three and three is six.	$3 + 3 = 6$ $6 - 3 = 3$
2 triangles and an extra line on a drawing. How many line segments? 3 plus 3 is 6 and 1 more is 7. One triangle is erased. How many line segments left?	Add one to make a double plus one.	Double plus one: three and three is six and one more is seven.	$4 + 3 = 7$ or $3 + 4 = 7$ $7 - 3 = 4$
One car had 4 tires and another car had 4 tires. There were 8 tires.	Build the first number on the top row and double it by building it again in the second row. (Notice the negative space makes this ten-grid also say $8 + 2 = 10$.)	Double: four and four is eight.	$4 + 4 = 8$ $8 - 4 = 4$
2 cars with 4 tires and a unicycle. 9 tires.	This is double plus one.	Double plus one: four and four is eight and one more is nine.	$4 + 4 + 1 = 9$ or $5 + 4 = 9$ $9 - 5 = 4$

Figure 5.2 *Building and verbalizing* (continued)

Contextualize	Build and visualize	Verbalize	Represent
5 boys on the red team. 5 boys on the blue team. 10 boys.	Build the first number on the top row and double it by building it again in the second row.	Double: five and five is ten.	$5 + 5 = 10$
One more boy comes to the blue team, now there are 11.	Build the double plus one by using a second ten grid and splitting the double between two grids.	Double plus one: five and five is ten and one more is eleven.	$5 + 6 = 11$
6 volleyball players on one team and 6 on the other.		Double: six and six is twelve.	$6 + 6 = 12$
1 referee. 13 people on the volleyball court.		Double plus one: six and six is twelve and one more is thirteen.	$6 + 7 = 13$

Figure 5.2 *Building and verbalizing* (continued)

Doubles and Even Numbers

It is important to note that doubling a number always yields an even number. In this way children can recognize that every even number can be a double (or divided into two equal groups). To emphasize this concept, fill in a chart like the one shown in Figure 5.3 and ask, "What patterns do you see?"

Number	Double it	Sum	Take half the sum	Difference
1	1 + 1	2	2 − 1	1
2	2 + 2	4	4 − 2	2
3	3 + 3	6	6 − 3	3
4	4 + 4	8	8 − 4	4

Figure 5.3 *Doubles, sums, and differences*

Identifying What Still Needs to be Learned

Consider the addition fact chart shown in Figure 5.4 that shows all of the one-digit addition facts as sums of two numbers. In a table like this, students see only the incredibly scary task of figuring out how to memorize 100 bits of information. However, looked at more carefully, and with the individualized support of teachers, this chart can help students recognize which facts they have mastery or fluency over and how the commutative property reduces the memory load by half. Over time, by circling each of the known facts, students gradually recognize how few facts actually remain troublesome.

We often provide each student with this chart and use it to check off or shade in fluently known facts—those that are retrievable in two seconds or less. Think of the relief on the part of a struggling student who realizes that adding 0 doesn't change the number and how easy it is to "add on" one or two. This allows a student to record mastery of the top three rows and leftmost three columns, for a whopping 51 of the 100 facts!

The central lower diagonal now represents all of the doubles, the doubles plus one, doubles minus one, doubles plus two, and doubles minus two, or an additional

0 + 0	0 + 1	0 + 2	0 + 3	0 + 4	0 + 5	0 + 6	0 + 7	0 + 8	0 + 9
1 + 0	1 + 1	1 + 2	1 + 3	1 + 4	1 + 5	1 + 6	1 + 7	1 + 8	1 + 9
2 + 0	2 + 1	2 + 2	2 + 3	2 + 4	2 + 5	2 + 6	2 + 7	2 + 8	2 + 9
3 + 0	3 + 1	3 + 2	3 + 3	3 + 4	3 + 5	3 + 6	3 + 7	3 + 8	3 + 9
4 + 0	4 + 1	4 + 2	4 + 3	4 + 4	4 + 5	4 + 6	4 + 7	4 + 8	4 + 9
5 + 0	5 + 1	5 + 2	5 + 3	5 + 4	5 + 5	5 + 6	5 + 7	5 + 8	5 + 9
6 + 0	6 + 1	6 + 2	6 + 3	6 + 4	6 + 5	6 + 6	6 + 7	6 + 8	6 + 9
7 + 0	7 + 1	7 + 2	7 + 3	7 + 4	7 + 5	7 + 6	7 + 7	7 + 8	7 + 9
8 + 0	8 + 1	8 + 2	8 + 3	8 + 4	8 + 5	8 + 6	8 + 7	8 + 8	8 + 9
9 + 0	9 + 1	9 + 2	9 + 3	9 + 4	9 + 5	9 + 6	9 + 7	9 + 8	9 + 9

Figure 5.4 *Addition facts table*

twenty-nine facts! That's eighty facts that are all retrievable not just by memory but by applying two straightforward strategies that both build from counting, counting on, and counting back.

Next we turn to the remaining eight "add 9 facts," which we believe are accessible by adding ten and counting back one. That leaves, again to the great relief of students who might feel overwhelmed by the magnitude of "memorizing all those facts," just 3 + 6, 3 + 7, 3 + 8, 4 + 7, 4 + 8, and 5 + 8 and their reverses. These facts lend themselves to a "making ten" strategy that helps bring students to fluency as well.

Obviously, there are additional strategies that many students find comfortable to establish fluency with facts, but our point is to note the power of helping students delimit what is not yet mastered and keep track of the growing body of facts that are mastered.

■ Classroom Activities

As we have noted, learning is maximized when our students are consistently contextualizing, constructing, representing, verbalizing, visualizing, and justifying. The following activities reflect these processes. The key point we hope to reiterate is that fact mastery does not arise from mad minutes and speed sprints. Rather, continued attention to "How did you know that?" and "What strategy did your brain use?" and "Can you convince us that $4 + 7$ is 11?" are the elements of class discussions and tutorial work. The activities that follow are designed to provide both practice and opportunities to explain and justify.

Developing Facts from Five to Ten

Tallies, Fingers and Coins

Tallies, fingers and coins are three different, but easily accessible, representations that help build fluency with facts from five to ten. Consider asking a class of six and seven year olds: "Show me how old you are with fingers. Now show me your age with tallies. Now can you show it with nickels and pennies?"

Asking students to describe how each representation of their age is the same encourages seeing, saying, and representing that $5 + 2$ is the same as 7 (see Figure 5.5). Repeat with "show me" using the three representations to first establish $5 + 1$, $5 + 2$, $5 + 3$, $5 + 4$, and $5 + 5$, and then to build from 5 to establish or reinforce $6 + 2$, $6 + 3$, $6 + 4$, $7 + 2$, $7 + 3$, $8 + 2$ (see Figure 5.6).

Although our focus here is on facts from five to ten, using tallies and nickels and pennies for these facts sets a foundation for helping to build fluency with

Figure 5.5 *Showing 5 + 2 in different ways*

bigger numbers. For example, ask students to "Use tallies and coins to show six and eight and convince your partner that 6 + 8 is 14." As shown, we are helping students convert 6 + 8 to 5 + 5 + 4 or 10 + 4 (see Figure 5.7).

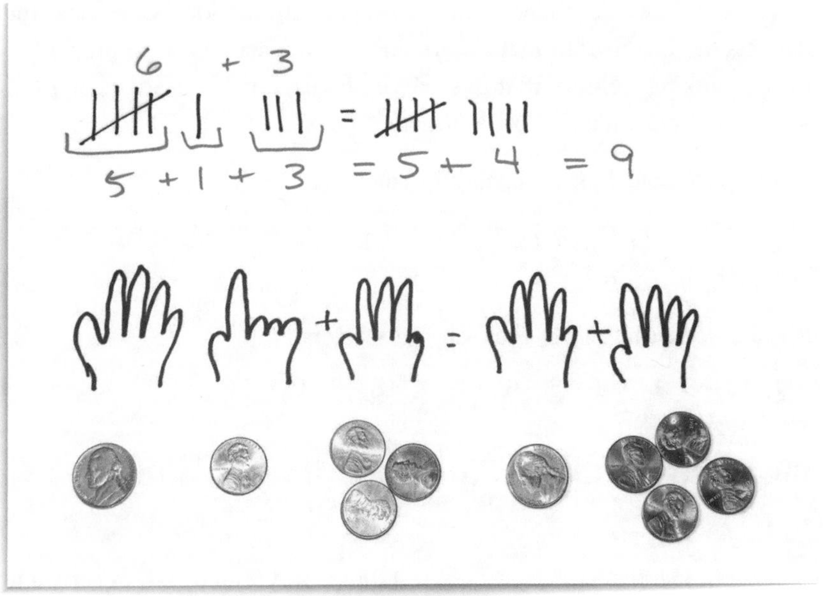

Figure 5.6 *Showing 6 + 3 in different ways*

Figure 5.7 *Showing 6 + 8 in different ways*

Chunking by Fives

"Chunking by fives" refers to knowing and using the fives inside numbers to add or subtract. For example: 8 is 5 + 3 and 7 is 5 + 2 so 8 + 7 must be 5 + 5 + 3 + 2 or 10 + 5 or 15. Similarly, 15 − 7 can be thought of as 15 − 5, which we know is 10, minus 2 more to get to 8, because the 7 was decomposed into 5 and 2.

In this activity provide students, one at a time, with the following facts, and direct students to "Use fives to make this sum or difference easier. Be prepared to explain your thinking." Notice that this activity focuses on what are recognized as the most troublesome addition and subtraction facts.

Sums where chunking by fives supports mastery:

6 + 6, 6 + 7, 6 + 8, 6 + 9, 7 + 6, 7 + 7, 7 + 8, 7 + 9, 8 + 6, 8 + 7

8 + 8, 8 + 9, 9 + 6, 9 + 7, 9 + 8, 9 + 9

Differences where chunking by fives supports mastery:

12 − 7, 13 − 8, 14 − 9, 15 − 6, 15 − 7, 15 − 8, 15 − 9

Doubling and Doubling Plus and Minus 1 and 2

Double It

This is a game to help teach the concept of doubles and how to recognize doubles on number cubes.

Materials needed: two number cubes (1–6 or 4–9) per player

Each player has ten rolls, but can only keep that quantity if doubles is rolled. After ten rolls each player totals their doubles and reports their total. The player with the highest total wins that round. Players play five rounds of ten rolls to see who wins.

Neighbor Numbers

Doubles plus one is sometimes a hard concept to understand. One way to think of it is by using a number line to see "neighbor numbers." Numbers that are next to one another on the number line are "neighbor numbers" and their sum is double the lesser number, plus one (or double the greater number, minus one).

Here is one way to explore this with students. Have children look at 7 and 8 on a number line.

> *What do you notice about them?* (7 is odd, 8 is even. 8 is more than 7.)
>
> *How could you add them?* (I see 7 and 7 is 14 and one more is 15.)
>
> *What do you notice about the sum?* (It is one more than a double; it is odd.)

Repeat with more examples, such as 8 and 9 or 9 and 10.

Have students complete a chart such as the one in Figure 5.8. For students who are ready to move beyond 10, have them explore more pairs. Discuss the patterns they see in the chart.

Neighbor numbers	Double the lower.	Add one to the second addend.	What is the sum?	Even or Odd?
7, 8	7 + 7 = 14	7 + 8	7 + 8 = 15	Odd
8, 9	8 + 8 = 16	8 + 9	8 + 9 = 17	Odd
9, 10	9 + 9 = 18	9 + 10	9 + 10 = 19	Odd

Figure 5.8 *Neighbor numbers*

Developing Fluency with Facts to 20

Make a Teen

There are many different ways to represent teen numbers: numerals, words, tallies, expanded notation, dimes and pennies, base ten materials, craft stick bundles, and ten-grids. Regardless of the specific representation, it is essential to emphasize that all teen numbers will always be the same as 10 + ___.

Create sets of teen cards for the teen numbers. Figure 5.9 shows a set of such cards for thirteen.

Provide the following directions:

1. *Draw a teen numeral card.*

2. *Build the quantity using two ten-frames (or whatever representation you want students to use. See Figure 5.10).*

3. *Convince your partner that what you have built is accurate.*

4. *Continue until you and your partner have each built each number from 11–19.*

Figure 5.9 *Make a teen*

Figure 5.10 *Making a teen*

Calendar Discussions

During calendar discussions or number talks, it is always good to point out teen numbers as special and ask some questions:

> *What addends make this number?*
>
> *Is it a double or a double plus one?*
>
> *What number is doubled?*
>
> *How do you know?*
>
> *Can you write this number as ten plus some other number?*

Strategy Discussions or "How Do You Know That?"

This is where great number sense and practice with making ten really pays off. If you know that 7 + 3, 8 + 2, and 9 + 1 all add to 10, you can decompose the second addend in a pair such as 9 + 4 to make a 10 (see Figure 5.11).

Practicing the language of this strategy is what builds fluency and flexibility. Listen as students tell how they know the answer to 9 and 4:

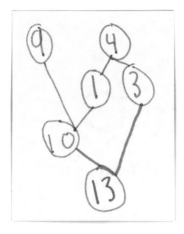

Figure 5.11 *Showing 9 + 4 in different ways*

- Dade explains: *I know 9 + 4 = 13 because 4 is 3 and 1 and I can add my 9 to the 1 and get 10 + 3 and that is the same as 9 + 4.*
- Jackson drew a picture with a number bond.
- Max drew a ten-grid with nine filled and one left over; he then filled the empty spot with another color dot and placed three dots on the side.

* * * * * * * *

As we move forward to discuss more complex multi-digit operations in the next chapter, bear in mind that those operations demand a deep understanding of small numbers along with place value concepts. The importance of deep understanding of and fluency with facts to 20 cannot be overstated.

Chapter 6

Developing Fluency Finding Sums and Differences

Thus far we have discussed parts and wholes, small numbers, and addition and subtraction to 5, 10, and 20. In this chapter we will extend the fluency discussion to sums and differences of larger numbers, beginning with numbers to 100 and then to three- and four-digit numbers. When these key topics are taught poorly, as rules that make no sense, without connections to place value, and when taught too quickly or too early, the first cries of "I don't get it!" and "I'm not good in math" begin to emerge. We have a long history of doing real damage to children—damage that can and must be avoided.

It is often argued that subtraction with regrouping is the first major conceptual hurdle of the elementary school mathematics curriculum. Whether called "carrying and borrowing," or "regrouping," or "decomposing," the basis of all addition and subtraction of two-, three-, and four-digit numbers is adding over tens and understanding place value—particularly, for example, that 18 tens is the same as 180 or 1 hundred and 8 tens, or that 76 is the same as 60 and 16 or 6 tens and 16 ones. It is important to note that place value is exactly what the name implies: being able to tell the value of a number by its place, understanding that the 7 in 375 is 7 tens or 70 and not just the "7 that lives in the tens place."

Fluency with finding sums and differences is *not* based on memorized rules like "cross out the 8 and make it a 7," but instead on the critical understanding that when adding and subtracting, one adds or subtracts hundreds and hundreds, tens and tens, and ones and ones, but sometimes it is necessary to compose or decompose the tens or hundreds based on place value understanding. These are the critical and underlying understandings that we will focus on in this chapter.

Key Ideas and Skills

One of the densest and most important standards within all of the K-5 *Common Core State Standards for Mathematics* (National Governors Association 2010) is the mouthful in grade 2 within the cluster "Use place value understanding and properties of operations to add and subtract" that reads:

> Add and subtract with 1000, using concrete models or drawings and strategies based on place value, properties of operations, and/or the relationship between addition and subtraction; relate the strategy to a written method. Understand that in adding and subtracting three-digit numbers, one adds or subtracts hundreds and hundreds, tens and tens, ones and ones; and sometimes it is necessary to compose or decompose tens or hundreds. (19)

Place value understandings undergird fluency finding sums and differences, and a number of important ideas, under the umbrella of place value, contribute mightily to numerical fluency: unitization, a deep understanding of the teen numbers, expanded notation, counting on and back by tens and hundreds, and using standard and alternative algorithms *with understanding*.

Unitization

Unitization is the idea that quantities can be bundled into a group, and that group becomes a unit itself. In particular, students need to master the fundamental notion that 10 ones can be bundled to become 1 ten, 10 tens can be bundled to become 1 hundred, etc. While the language is easy to state, understanding the concept is more challenging. Very young children are used to counting by ones. Changing the counting unit to tens or hundreds requires processing time.

While students are typically provided many opportunities to convert numbers between standard form and expanded notation, it is rare that students get enough opportunities to master and justify such equivalences as:

10 tens = 1 hundred

100 tens = 1 thousand

10 hundreds = 1 thousand

160 = 16 tens

67 = 6 tens + 7 ones = 5 tens + 17 ones

254 = 2 hundreds + 5 tens + 4 ones = 1 hundred + 15 tens + 4 ones =
1 hundred + 14 tens + 14 ones

Activities that involve grouping and counting help students build this understanding.

Comprehending the Teen Numbers (11–19)

First-grade teachers often call the teen numbers the nightmare numbers. Learning to count using teen numbers is often very confusing because when spoken, the teen numbers sound backwards. That is, fifteen sounds like "five-ten" to a small child, unlike twenty-five, which matches its numeral more clearly.

Second, while children in kindergarten are often exposed to counting teen numbers and seeing "a group of ten and some ones," unitizing requires them to see 15 as 1 ten and 5 ones instead of one group of ten and five. This may seem like a slight difference, but this new understanding of "a ten" (rather than "a group of ten things") leads to numerical fluency with larger numbers.

Contrast our teen numbering system with Chinese Mandarin, in which the number names for ten, eleven, twelve, thirteen, and fourteen, etc., translate roughly into one-ty, one-ty one, one-ty two, one-ty three, and one-ty four, etc. Alas, how much easier it is to make sense of these teen numbers when their names actually match their place value, instead of being stuck with "eleven" and "twelve" for starters!

Expanded Notation

Along with unitizing comes the idea that numbers greater than ten can be expressed in expanded notation (also called expanded form). One writes a number as the sum of the value of each digit, for example, $17 = 10 + 7$, and $3,458 = 3000 + 400 + 50 + 8$.

There are three important ideas to remember about expanded notation:

1. Expanding a teen number is essential to implementing the "make a ten strategy": $9 + 6 = 10 + 5 = 15$.

2. Accurately representing expanded notation, as in $778 = 700 + 70 + 8$, demonstrates understanding of the value of each place in the number.

3. When adding or subtracting larger numbers, a deep understanding of expanded notation enhances mental math. For example, if we can "see" 5 hundreds and 3 hundreds in $534 + 300$, finding the sum of 834 is straightforward. Similarly, $534 - 300$ quickly becomes 234 when we "see" 5 hundreds minus 3 hundreds.

Counting On and Back by Tens, Hundreds, and Thousands

Counting forward and backward by tens, hundreds, thousands, and eventually millions takes important place value understanding. Counting on and off the ten (that is, counting 10, 20, 30 . . . or 17, 27, 37 . . .) is basic to being able to add and subtract multi-digit numbers. Students count up orally by tens from 0 or 10, but counting forwards and backwards starting with any decade number, including the numbers in the hundreds and thousands, leads to deeper understanding. This idea is codified in the *Common Core State Standards for Mathematics* (National Governors Association 2010), where children are expected to identify 10 more or less, 100 more or less, and 1000 more or less than a given number.

Counting on and counting back by tens when the initial number is *not* a multiple of ten (13, 23, 33 . . . or 73, 63, 53 . . . versus 10, 20, 30 . . . or 70, 60, 50 . . .) can be a difficult skill. Particular attention needs to be paid to going over the decade mark (that is, from 94 to 104 or from 206 to 196). This can also be particularly challenging to students. Fluency with adding and subtracting tens and hundreds from any number is very helpful for adding and subtracting mentally.

Alternative Standard Algorithms

It is important to note that we are very strong supporters of the K–8 *Common Core State Standards for Mathematics* (National Governors Association 2010). We believe that nearly all of the ideas proposed in this book are completely aligned with both the letter and the spirit of the Common Core with one glaring exception. We strongly disagree with the wording and intent of two standards:

Grade 4: Fluently add and subtract multi-digit whole numbers using the standard algorithm. (29)

Grade 5: Fluently multiply and divide whole numbers using the standard algorithm. (35)

"*The* standard algorithm" is a serious misnomer. There may be one more typical or more popular algorithm in the United States, but that does not make it *the* standard approach or the only approach, and other countries fare very well with other alternative algorithms. As we shall see, there are several "standard" algorithms that are just as efficient, but far more accessible, than the so-called one and only standard algorithm of yore. To support this focus on alternative, but still standard, algorithms, we draw on our own experience and the incredibly helpful work of our colleagues Karen Fuson and Sybilla Beckmann on what exactly constitute "standard algorithms" (2012).

> There is nothing wrong with standard algorithms, even with the so-called one and only standard algorithm, for each of the four operations. These procedures that many have memorized and used for decades are efficient ways to compute sums, differences, products, and quotients. However, they are also vestiges from an era before there were calculators and the Amazon Alexa and other voice-controlled intelligent personal assistants. Beyond two or three digits these algorithms are less and less important today, and other algorithms make the development of numerical fluency much more accessible to many who in the past struggled mightily with subtraction involving regrouping and with two-digit divisor long division.

Our greatest concern with the notion of the one and only standard algorithm is how it fails to support necessary differentiation among the learning needs of our students. Watch a number talk done well, and we marvel at the different ways students work with numbers and arrive at correct answers. Then observe these same students constrained to doing pencil and paper mathematics in only one way. It just doesn't make sense to us or to our students!

Addition Algorithms

Figure 6.1 shows five different algorithms for addition. Algorithm A represents the so-called standard algorithm, "carrying the one" every time we get a teen sum. Algorithms B and C both use partial sums; B starts with the ones and moves to the hundreds, while C uses the same approach except for moving from the hundreds to the ones. Not only do approaches B and C avoid the "carry the one" feature and lay

Figure 6.1 *Standard addition algorithms*

groundwork that carries over to multiplying with partial products (see Chapter 9), these two alternative algorithms are based on simple place value thinking: 7 ones and 8 ones are 15 ones or 15, 4 tens and 6 tens are 10 tens or 100, and 3 hundreds and 2 hundreds are simply 5 hundreds or 500. Algorithm D is similar to the "standard" Algorithm A, but instead of inserting the little 1s, we change the digit by one. That is, since 7 plus 8 is 15 or 5 ones and 1 ten, instead of inserting the little 1 before the 4 to represent 4 tens plus 1 ten, we simply increase the 4 to a 5 to account for the extra 10 from the 15. Finally, in Algorithm E we simply "add the one," which we understand to be 10, at the bottom of each column so that the 15 and the 11 are created by digits that are much closer to each other than in the so-called standard algorithm. While there is obviously no good reason to expect students to be fluent with all of these approaches, it is just as foolish to expect that all students will feel most comfortable with the so-called standard algorithm rather than one of these equally valid alternatives.

Subtraction Algorithms

Similarly, Figure 6.2 shows five different standard algorithms for subtraction. Algorithm A represents the often unwieldy "cross out and borrow" approach so alien to so many students and so ignored in many other countries. Algorithms B and C—one moving from left to right and the other from right to left respectively—rename each digit in the minuend so that there is enough value in each column to subtract. That is, in order to have enough tens and ones, students rename 347 to 2 hundreds, 13 tens, and 17 ones. Algorithm D is common in Eastern Europe and is often called the "add ten add ten" strategy. Note that since there are not enough ones to subtract 8 from 7, we add 10 to the top by changing 347 to 3 hundreds, 4 tens and 17 ones. But since we added 10 to the top, we add 10 to the bottom by changing the 6 tens to 7 tens. Notice that all we are doing is getting enough ones by adding 10 in two different ways and in two different places. The process repeats by adding 10 tens to the 4 tens on the top and 1 hundred to the 2 hundreds on the bottom. All that this approach of adding 10 and adding 10 has done is to convert the original problem to 3 hundreds, 14 tens, and 17 ones minus 3 hundreds, 7 tens, and 8 ones, and since we have actually added 110 to both numbers, the difference does not change! Finally, Algorithm E records a counting-on strategy. (We'll see a related partial quotients strategy for division in Chapter 9.) As with addition, there is obviously no good reason to expect students to be fluent with all of these approaches, nor for all students to master the so-called standard algorithm.

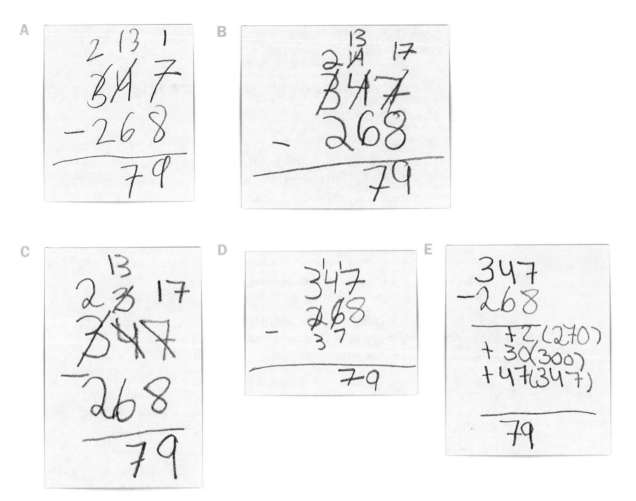

Figure 6.2 *Standard subtraction algorithms*

■ Classroom Activities

As we have emphasized, learning is maximized when our students are consistently contextualizing, constructing, representing, verbalizing, visualizing, and justifying. Once again, the following activities reflect these processes. Rather than naked practice, we urge the use of contexts such as menus, price lists, and other sources of accessible and interesting data. In addition to numerical representations, students need blocks, place value mats, and pictures to help them make sense of composing and decomposing tens and hundreds. And students need to be asked "Why?" and

"Can you convince us?" to encourage them to verbalize and justify their strategies and their understandings and misunderstandings.

Activities to Support Place-Value Understanding

How Many in the Bag or Jar?

Children love to guess how many and then see how close their guesses were. Use "counting jars" or "counting bags" filled with beans or macaroni or beads or cubes over the course of the school year, increasing the number of objects as students move from tens to hundreds to thousands.

1. Hold up a bag of plastic cubes or a bag of lima beans or a box of macaroni.

2. Ask students to think of a number that they know is too low for the number of cubes or beans or elbows and write that number on their whiteboards. Ask students to justify why they think their guess is too low.

3. Then ask students to think of a number that they know is too high for the number of cubes or beans or elbows and write that number on their whiteboards. Again, ask students to justify why they think their guess is too high.

4. Having discussed guesses that are too large and too small, ask students to think for a minute and estimate the actual number of cubes, beans or elbows in the bag or box and write that number on their whiteboards.

5. Use a flip chart to record (in no particular order) the students' estimates. This is a great opportunity to ask students to identify the largest and smallest estimates, or to ask if they want to revise their estimates.

> The set of estimates can also be used as a set of statistics and placed on a number line for additional exploration into how the estimates are clumped or spread out.

6. Now count out ten cubes or beans or elbow macaroni and place them into a pile that all students can see. Ask students to use this "reference pile of ten" to revise their estimates. This often leads to a great discussion of how and why students made their revisions.

7. Finally, it's time to actually count the number of objects, and for this we need small condiment cups (that hold a few more than ten objects), plastic cups (that hold a few more than one hundred objects), and large bottles or jars (that hold a few more than one thousand objects). The entire class sorts the objects into tens in the small condiment cups, pours the objects from ten of these condiment cups into the plastic cups to start recording hundreds, and, if there are more than a thousand objects, pours the objects from ten cups of one hundred into the large bottle or jar to show one thousand. If you have used connecting cubes, students can join them to create 10-sticks and then 100-rods.

Note that it is never a matter of whose estimate was closest to the actual value, but rather a matter of how close our estimates were or were not, and of physically and systematically working with ones, tens, and hundreds, and recording the final actual number of objects.

Here are some of the questions we have asked students as they estimated and recorded:

> *Which estimates are the greatest? Smallest?*
>
> *Which estimate is one more than 69?*
>
> *Which estimate is ten less than 123?*
>
> *Which estimates have the digits in order from least to greatest?*
>
> *Which estimate is the same as 5 dimes, 1 nickel, and 3 pennies?*

After the actual number is determined:

> *Which estimates were closest to the actual number?*
>
> *Which were far from the actual number? About how far?*
>
> *How did sorting the objects into tens and then hundreds make it easier to count them all?*

How Else Can We Express this Number?

Write a multi-digit number in standard and expanded notation, and challenge students to come up with other ways to represent that number using different quantities of tens and ones. For example:

> *Let's take 91, which we know can be written as 90 + 1. How else can we express 91 with tens and ones?* Possible answers: 80 + 11 or 70 + 21.

The activity gets far more interesting with three-digit numbers:

> Today's number is 438, which we know can be written as 400 + 30 +
> 8. What other sums of hundreds, tens, and ones are equivalent to 438?
> Possible answers: 400 + 20 + 18 or 300 + 130 + 8 or 300 + 120 + 18.

For students who struggle with finding correct equivalents, base ten blocks are excellent tools for representing and seeing the equivalence among 4 hundreds, 3 tens, 8 ones; 4 hundreds, 2 tens, 18 ones; 3 hundreds, 13 tens, 8 ones; and 3 hundreds, 12 tens, 18 ones.

Adding and Subtracting Tens

Count on Tens and Ones

Basic Game: Count on Tens

Materials needed: two number cubes and recording sheet

Use two cubes, one labeled 10, 20, 30, 10, 20, 30 and one labeled 0, 1, 2, 3, 4, 5. Player 1 tosses the 10, 20, 30 cube and says that number. Next they toss the 0–5 cube and count on that many tens. They then write and tell the resulting number. Player 2 does the same. The players compare their numbers. The one with the smaller number wins that round and gets a check mark. (Students can also play for the larger number.) Players play seven rounds. The player with the most checks wins.

Variation: Count on Tens and Ones

In this variation, the cubes are labeled 10, 20, 30, 40, 50, 60 and 0, 1, 2, 3, 4, 5. Students roll both cubes and write the resulting number (so if a player rolls 40 and 3, the resulting number is 43).

Variation: Count Up by Tens

In this variation, the cubes are the same as in Count on Tens and Ones. The players roll both cubes and say the resulting number (e.g., 50 + 2 is 52). They then roll the 0–5 cube again and count up that many tens from the starting number.

Closest to 100

Materials needed:
two number cubes
one 100-chart
two counters of different colors or a penny and a nickel

Player 1 tosses a 10, 20, 30, 40, 50, 60 cube and the 1, 2, 3, 4, 5, 6 cube and says the number (e.g., 20 and 6 gives 26) and places their counter on a 100-chart. Then they toss the 1–6 cube and move forward or backward that many tens to get as close to 100 as possible without going over. If the player rolled 4, for instance, they could move forward to 66. But if 66 were the first roll and 5 the second, the player would have to go back to 16. Player 2 repeats the same process and the winner of the round is the player who ends up closest to 100. Players play for five rounds. The player closest to 100 in the most rounds wins.

Practice with Addition and Subtraction

Problem Bank: Comparison Subtraction

Comparison subtraction problems are some of the most confusing for young children. Drawing pictures is a strategy that helps students determine what they know and what they need to find out.

Here are some problems to foster understanding and fluency with comparative subtraction.

1. Ms. Thornton has 18 cents. Ms. Meyer has 7 cents. How much more money does Ms. Thornton have than Ms. Meyer?

   Students can use a picture here to compare the amounts and look for the difference or how many more.

2. There were 18 boys with light blue shirts on. There were 10 boys with dark blue shirts on. Which color shirt had more? How many more light blue shirts than dark blue shirts were there?

   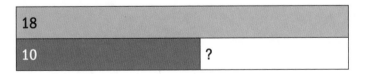

   Students can use bars to compare and look at differences.

3. I was at the park. I saw 18 brown ducks and 12 white ducks. How many more brown ducks were there than white ducks?

4. Tom read 47 books. Sam read 15 books. How many fewer books did Sam read than Tom?

5. Ms. Auritt made 25 cookies. Ms. Brown made 47 cookies. How many more cookies did Ms. Brown make than Ms. Auritt?

6. At the pond, there were 11 yellow butterflies. There were 6 orange butterflies. There were 20 frogs. How many fewer orange butterflies were there than yellow butterflies?

7. There were 18 girls swimming in the pool. There were 7 boys swimming in the pool. How many fewer boys than girls were swimming in the pool?

8. Ms. Merrow was at the beach. She saw 63 fish. She saw 19 dolphins. How many fewer dolphins than fish did she see?

9. In summer, Sara read 7 books, Jan read 10 more books than Sara, and Jim read 8 fewer books than Jan. How many books did Jan read? How many books did Jim read? How many books did the three friends read all together?

Milking Engaging Data

Use the internet to find sets of engaging data that your students can relate to. For example, Figure 6.3 lists the populations of the five largest cities in Nebraska.

These questions might be posed to students:

About how many people live in these five cities?

Exactly how many people lived in these five cities in 2010?

How many more people live in Omaha than in Lincoln?

How many more people live in Omaha than in the other four cities combined?

Make up and solve a problem based on these data. Switch problems with your neighbor.

City	Population
Omaha	408,958
Lincoln	258,379
Bellevue	50,137
Grand Island	48,520
Kearney	30,787

Figure 6.3 *Population of five largest Nebraska cities, 2010 (Source: US Census 2010)*

Pick-a-Number Games

We and our students are great fans of Pick-a-Number Games, in which students place selected digits in number spaces to get the largest sums or differences, smallest sums or differences, or a sum or difference closest to a given number. We use 0–9 number cards and assorted game boards. Here is one example, using two-digit numbers to find the greatest sum. Use the game board shown in Figure 6.4.

Randomly draw four digit cards, one at a time. Tell students that they must place each card in a box on the game board as you draw it, and once they've placed a digit, they cannot move it. Their goal is to make the *greatest* possible sum. After drawing all four digit cards, have students find and share their sums. Discuss why the "winning" arrangement of digits produced the greatest sum. If there is a greater possible sum than any student found, discuss how the digits could have been arranged to make it.

Other variations include finding the least possible sum, the greatest or least possible difference, a sum closest to 100, a difference closest to 20, etc. For beginning or struggling students, you can use the sum and difference of a two-digit and a one-digit number. For a challenge, consider using three-digit numbers.

Figure 6.4 *Pick-a-Number*

PART
THREE

Developing Multiplication and Division Fluency

Chapter 7

Giving Meaning to Multiplication and Division

We asked a class of third graders "What is multiplication?" Here is some of what we heard from the students:

Times tables

The problems with an X

Skip-counting

A fast way to add

Like three times seven is twenty-one

Counting by groups

Having remainders

Some of these answers contain parts of the meaning of multiplication. Others reflect confusion between multiplication and division. They remind us that many children receive only a brief introduction to multiplication and division and then the focus turns immediately to learning their "times tables" or multiplication facts with speed and accuracy. Other children learn to listen and tell stories about things in equal groups and record number sentences that involve using the times sign and discover that multiplication can be a quicker way to add. Others realize that if they can skip-count by twos, threes, fives, and tens, they can multiply. Still others experience the idea of making equal groups and telling how many are in each group. These children are developing fluency with multiplication and division through problems and contexts, using representations such as arrays and area models, verbalizing, visualizing, describing, and justifying. Our goal in this chapter is to discuss and model practical ways to develop the foundational understanding of multiplication and division as a necessary prerequisite for learning facts and multiplying and dividing larger numbers.

The concepts of multiplication and division develop over time as students experience a range of situations in which they combine equal-sized groups (How many chairs are in 6 rows that each have 8 chairs?) or divide into equal-sized groups (If you have 48 chairs, how many rows can be set up with 8 chairs in each row? *or* How many chairs will be in each row if there are 8 rows?).

Consider that one of the most common questions heard in grades 3 through 5 classrooms when students are working on word problems is "Do I multiply or divide?" We all know that when we answer that question and just tell our students whether to multiply or divide, we have taken from them the heart of understanding operations. Alternatively, effective teachers know to ask questions like "Can you sketch a picture of this situation?" or "Can you tell us whether the numbers in the problem are factors or products—that is, are they parts or are they totals?" This is why devoting quality time to the meaning of multiplication and division is so important.

Key Ideas and Skills

We believe that the meanings of multiplication and division are supported by the following ideas.

Understanding the Meaning of Multiplication

Multiplication is a mathematical operation, like addition and subtraction, and describes real action using objects, and then numbers, to put together equal groups and find the total. Counting multiple items in groups by ones is a beginning, followed by skip-counting by equal groups, and later using the number line to represent the skipping as equal jumps on the number line. Arrays and area models are also powerful tools for developing an understanding of the meaning of multiplication.

Understanding the Meaning of Division

Division, the inverse operation of multiplication, is another mathematical operation that can be used to find the number of groups or the amount in each group. Division arises in stories when either the number of groups or the quantity in each group is unknown. (Keeping track of the difference between the number of objects *in* each group and the number *of* groups is often the source of great confusion when students are first learning about division.) Division can also be thought of as repeated subtraction, moving backwards on a number line in equal jumps. As with multiplication, arrays and area models are again powerful tools for developing the meaning of division.

Part-Whole Relationships

Just as students have learned about part-whole relationships between addends and sums in addition and subtraction, with the support of arrays and area models students learn about the similar factor-product relationships in multiplication and division. They build the critical understanding that when a and b are factors and c is the product, then $a \times b = c$, and it follows that $b \times a$ is also equal to c, $c \div b$ must be a, and $c \div a$ must be b.

Arrays and Rectangular Area Models

Arrays are a powerful way to build, visualize, verbalize, represent, and justify multiplication. Discussing rows and columns helps students see equal groups. Organizing counters in equal rows and columns is an efficient strategy for connecting repeated addition to multiplication. Furthermore, arrays provide an opportunity to explore the commutative property for multiplication. Lastly, arrays connect the measurement of the area of rectangles to multiplication and division.

Reading arrays provides an opportunity to understand the relationship between factors and products. For example, an array that has four columns of three rows has twelve items in all. 4 and 3 are factors, and 12 is the product (see Figure 7.1).

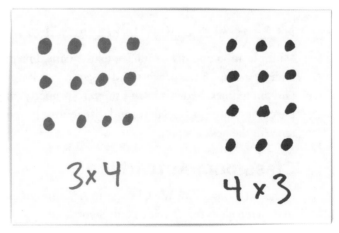

Figure 7.1 *Arrays for 3 × 4 and 4 × 3*

Four groups of three and three groups of four can easily be seen in the same array to help students visualize the commutative property. Rotating the array (changing the order of the factors) does not change the product.

The study of arrays leads to conceptual understanding that the area of a rectangle can be represented and found by multiplying two numbers together. As we'll see in Chapter 9, area models become important supports for building fluency with the multiplication and division algorithms.

Multiplication and Division Stories

Understanding when and why to multiply or divide emerges from stories or situations and connecting the stories (words) with representations (objects and pictures). These stories are translated to numbers using symbols, × and ÷, as a kind of shorthand. But it is important to make sure that students understand what the results of that shorthand mean in context.

This can be especially tricky in interpreting quotients with remainders. For example, consider the simple problem $27 \div 5$. When we ask how many pies can you buy when you have $27 and pies cost $5 each, the answer is 5. When we ask how many taxicabs are needed when 27 people go to a restaurant and each taxi holds 5 people, the answer is 6. When we share $27 equally among 5 people, each person gets $5.40. And when we share 27 apples among 5 children, each child gets 5 apples and there are 2 left, or 3 children get 5 apples each and two children get 6 apples each. The same 27 is divided by 5, but depending upon the context, there are four or five different, but entirely correct, answers!

Properties of Multiplication and Division

Multiplication and division have mathematical properties that encourage the understanding of the process and assist in developing fluency: the identity property (anything times 1 equals itself), the zero property (anything times 0 equals 0), and the commutative, associative, and distributive properties. We will discuss these more in the next chapter.

■ Classroom Activities

As has been noted for the Classroom Activities in each chapter so far, our hope is to provide ideas for activities that incorporate the six processes of contextualizing, constructing, representing, verbalizing, visualizing, and justifying. Each of these processes is important to help students develop a deep and lasting understanding of the meaning of the operations of multiplication and division and how these operations are related as inverse operations.

Developing Multiplication and Division Understanding

Modeling Stories

Provide students with counters or other materials to model a multiplication situation as you describe it. Ask students to listen carefully as you read the story. Ask students to tell you what the story is about. Then read the story a second time and ask students to use their counters or a drawing to represent the story. As students work, circulate to see whether they are accurately representing the situation and how they go about answering the questions. When someone is struggling, one good option is to ask that student to work with a partner to create and justify their models.

Here are some stories that model different big ideas in multiplication. The first addresses the fundamental idea of equal groups; students can see both numbers and know what to multiply:

A man had 3 cages with 2 bunnies in each cage. How many bunnies did he have?

The second story calls on prior knowledge (the number of sides in a triangle), and requires students to realize that they need information that isn't explicitly given:

Samantha uses craft sticks to make triangles for a design. If she made 6 designs, how many popsicle sticks did she use?

The third involves a missing factor, which is a more challenging situation for students to model:

There are 16 chicks at the farm and 2 can fit into a cage. How many cages do we need?

"Groups of . . . " Posters and Stories

Contextualizing multiplication is greatly enhanced by helping students identify things that come in groups in real life. Make posters or lists—or direct students to make their own posters—of objects that come in twos, threes, etc., and display them where students can see them. Use the lists for writing number stories and drawing pictures.

Before you begin this exercise, it is a nice connection to invite parents to collect ideas for the posters.

Dear Parent:

In the next few weeks we will be exploring "things that come in groups" as we begin our early exploration of multiplication and division. Please send examples of things that come in twos, threes, etc., that your child is familiar with. If you can, have your child bring in pictures to add to our class posters. We will use these posters to write number stories and draw pictures to understand these operations better.

We will be exploring one number every other day, starting with the number 2 on _____ (day).

Here are some ways to use these posters:

1. Have each student choose a group from a poster to write a story about. Encourage them to draw pictures to model their stories and include a solution. Here are some examples:

    I drew 4 squares. How many lines did I draw?

    To make some squares I drew 32 line segments. How many squares did I draw?

    We have 5 horses. How many legs are there?

    There were 30 legs among the horses on a farm. How many horses were there?

    I went to a restaurant with 6 tables. There were salt and pepper shakers on every table. How many salt and pepper shakers were there?

Make a booklet of these stories and use them for students to solve problems and model stories.

2. Students can also write "Guess My Number" riddles based on the posters:

> **I am not the number of eyes you have.**
>
> **I am more than the number of sides in a triangle.**
>
> **I am less than the number of days in the week.**
>
> **I am the same as the number of sides on a hexagon.**

Skip-Counting on a Number Line

Skip-counting means counting by skipping over the same number of numerals over and over. That is, skip-counting by 2 skips over one numeral each time to produce 2, 4, 6, 8, ... It is another example of the idea of equal groups and helps to solidify an understanding of multiplication. Recording equal skips or jumps on a number line helps students visualize this concept. Each jump is equidistant from the last, and the unit is defined by how many are in each jump. Each landing place visually represents the product of the number of jumps and the size of each jump. Likewise, division links to repeated subtraction.

Materials needed:

> *Sheet of paper with four number lines and fifty equidistant hash marks*
>
> *Markers*
>
> *Four groups of fifty counters (fifty beans or connecting cubes or random counters) for grouping*
>
> *12 x 18 construction paper for recording*

To launch this activity, group a small pile of beans by threes. Zero groups of three is zero, so model with students how to mark the number line at 0. Then one group of three is three, so write 3 in the appropriate place on the number line, show the jump from 0 to 3, and write $1 \times 3 = 3$ under the number line. The second jump represents two jumps or skips of three or $2 \times 3 = 6$, and the third jump is three more or $3 \times 3 = 9$. In this manner, students experience multiplication with concrete materials, jumps on a number line, number sentences, and physically and visually link multiplication to repeated addition.

Make four groups of students and assign each group a number between 2 and 5. Each group should make piles or groups with that number of objects in each group, making as many groups as possible with the counters they have. Students circle each group and then write the number of groups below them on the paper, along with matching multiplication sentences. See Figures 7.2 and 7.3 for examples. Students share their results until there are number lines for 2, 3, 4, and 5.

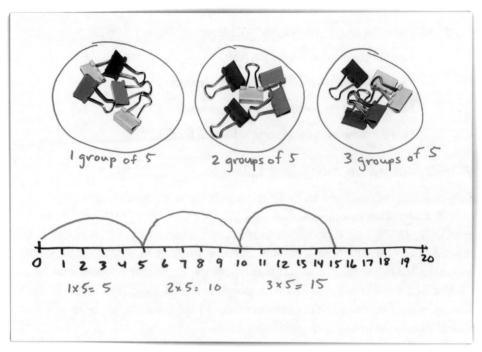

Figure 7.2 *Skip-counting by 5*

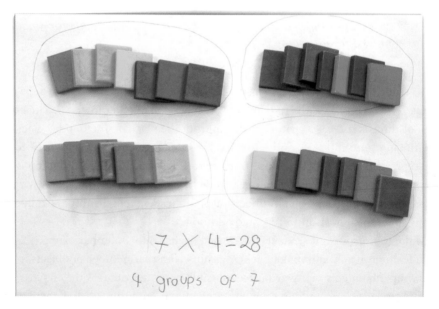

Figure 7.3 *Students can use tiles or other counters to make the groups.*

This is a great strategy to build understanding of one meaning of multiplication, but it is not a permanent solution for fact recall as it involves counting by groups each time. We will address fact strategies in the next chapter.

Contexts

Contextualizing is a critical process for students to build their understanding of the meaning of multiplication and division. Here are some ideas for contexts.

Chairs

Since chairs are often arranged in rows of the same number, they serve as a good context for strengthening an understanding of multiplication and division. Here are some helpful questions:

> Chairs are arranged in rows. Each row has the same number of chairs.
>
> There are 5 rows, with 8 chairs in each row. How many chairs are there in all? Why did you multiply or divide?
>
> 42 chairs are arranged in 6 rows. How many chairs are in each row? Why did you multiply or divide?
>
> We have 40 chairs in all, with 8 chairs in each row. How many rows do we have? Why did you multiply or divide?

Because the context is so accessible, this is a great place to have students create their own "chair" problems and share them with their partners. The chairs context also supports constructing and/or drawing pictures to represent various configurations.

Measurement Connections

The study of measurement is a wonderful way to increase students' understanding of multiplication and division as well as a great application of mathematics. Figure 7.4 links possible word problems with equivalent units for different types of measurement. After discussing one or two of the sample word problems, ask your students to use some of these equivalent measures to create, solve, and share with a partner other appropriate word problems.

Equivalent measures	Type of measurement	Sample word problems to differentiate between multiplication and division
1 foot equals 12 inches	Linear	The child is 3 feet 2 inches tall. How many inches?
2 cups equal a pint	Capacity/Volume	8 cups in the recipe. How many pints?
3 feet in a yard	Linear	A fence is 3 yards long. How many feet?
4 cups in a quart	Capacity/Volume	The punch recipe is for 3 quarts. How many cups?
5 pennies in a nickel	Money	10 nickels. How many pennies?
7 days in a week	Time	8 weeks. How many days?
8 ounces in a cup	Capacity/Volume	32 ounces. How many cups?
8 ounces in a half pound	Weight	Candy comes packed in half pound boxes. How many boxes in 40 ounces?
10 millimeters in a centimeter	Length	My key chain is 80 millimeters. How many centimeters?
10 centimeters in a meter	Length	The path is 12 meters. How many centimeters?

Figure 7.4 *Measurement ideas for problems*

Chapter 8

Developing Fluency with Multiplication and Division Facts

W e, and many of the elementary school teachers with whom we work, believe that mastery of multiplication and division facts is one of the greatest mathematical hurdles for many students and thus a powerful predictor of mathematical self-concept. It is therefore a topic that must be done right to ensure that all students get to maintain their self-confidence in their ability to do mathematics.

Here is a conversation very close to one we have both had with many fourth, fifth, and sixth graders:

Teacher: Do you know why you're getting extra help with math?

Student: Yes, because I do not do well in math.

Teacher: Can you be more specific about what part of math you don't do well in?

Student: Yes. I don't know my multiplication facts.

Teacher: That's pretty common. We hear that from a lot of students. Let's see what you do know about those multiplication facts. Okay?

Student: Okay.

Teacher: Let's start with two times two. Do you know what that is?

Student: Yes. two times two is four. That's an easy one.

Teacher: Okay. Let's make them harder. What is eight times one?

Student: That's eight because when you multiply something by one, it doesn't change.

Teacher: Great. So it appears that there are a lot of multiplication facts that you do in fact know.

Student: Maybe, but there are a lot I really don't know.

Teacher: Okay. Let's see if we can help find which facts you do know and which ones still need some work. Can you tell me what five times four is?

Student: Uhhh. Twenty?

Teacher: How did you get that?

Student: I knew that two fives were ten, so four fives had to be twenty. I also can do by fives pretty good I think.

Teacher: Okay. This is a great start. I'm going to get a zero times zero to ten times ten multiplication chart [see Figure 8.7 on page 122] and we're going to see how many multiplication facts you do know and how many you aren't sure of, and we'll work more on those.

In other words, students often know more than they think they do and yet the holes in their knowledge of facts seriously undermine their confidence. Helping students identify which facts they do in fact "own" and which facts are not "owned" can build confidence that all is not lost. In fact, "I stink in multiplication facts" often means struggles with only facts like 6×6, 6×7, 6×8, 6×9, 7×7, 7×8, 7×9, 8×8, 8×9 and 9×9. Just ten seriously troubling facts!

Key Ideas and Skills

The key ideas and skills for multiplication and division facts are similar to those for addition and subtraction facts: properties, relationships (doubling and skip-counting), thoughtful strategies, representations, and the realization that students really do know many facts, only a few of which are likely to be troublesome.

Properties

Understanding and using the properties of multiplication and division—particularly identities, inverses and the commutative and distributive properties—are very helpful for developing numerical fluency.

Identity and Zero Properties

The *identity property* of multiplication—the product of a number and 1 is the original number—builds a foundation for understanding multiplication facts for 1. While simple to teach as a rule, comprehending that one *set* of a number *is* that number is significant. Storytelling with groups of one is therefore important for giving meaning to multiplying by 1. For example, there is 1 group of 5 cows on the hill; Sarah has 1 box of 18 crayons; Jeremiah hit 2 home runs in 1 game, etc.

The *zero property* of multiplication is equally important to having a fluent knowledge of multiplication and division. This property states that any number multiplied by 0 will yield 0. This can be difficult to visualize. Representations can help (as shown in Figure 8.1).

This idea can also be represented with contextual situations, as in:

Boxes of cookies hold 8 cookies, but there are no boxes left. How many cookies are left?

There are 4 cookie boxes. They are all empty. How many cookies are there in the boxes?

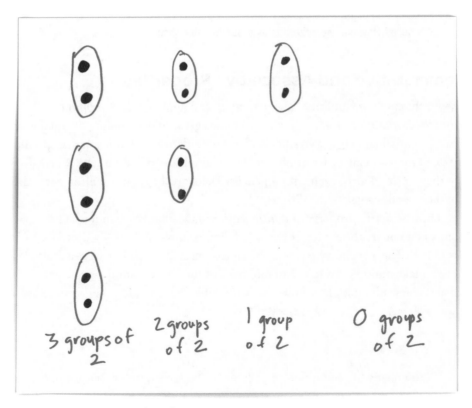

Figure 8.1 *Representing the zero property*

Children need the opportunity to tell stories using the property of zero and the property of one to completely and effectively use these strategies in their problem solving. For example:

1. Sarah has 6 bunnies. Each bunny has its own cage. How many cages are there? How many bunnies are in each cage? How can we write this as a number sentence?

2. Shawn has 17 marbles in 1 bag. How many marbles does he have? How many bags? How can we write this as a number sentence?

3. There are 7 seats on the bus. There are 7 people riding on the bus. How many seats are on the bus? How many riders are on the bus? How many people will be in each seat if there are an equal number of people in each seat? How can we write a number sentence to tell the story?

4. Jason picked pumpkins. He took 1 to each house. He went to 8 houses. How many pumpkins were picked? How many pumpkins were delivered to each house? How can we write this as a number sentence?

Commutative and Associative Properties

As was the case with addition, understanding and applying the *commutative property of multiplication* $(a \times b = b \times a)$ builds great understanding of equality and eases memory load. However, students need to understand that a story or situation may call for a specific order or picture. For example, 3 girls, each with 4 pencils, is not the same as 4 girls, each with 3 pencils. There are 12 total pencils in each case, but the visualization is quite different.

The *associative property of multiplication* states that you can multiply numbers no matter how they are grouped. For example, $2 \times 3 \times 4 = (2 \times 3) \times 4 = 2 \times (3 \times 4)$. The associative property becomes especially useful as we see multiples of two make multiples of four and multiples of four make multiples of eight. The same is true with multiples of three which double to make multiples of six: $2 \times 6 = 2 \times (3 \times 2) = 2 \times (2 \times 3) = (2 \times 2) \times 3 = 4 \times 3 = 12$.

Parentheses are often new to children in the lower grades, but they can understand that parentheses mean "do me first!"

The Distributive Property

It is difficult to overemphasize the importance of the distributive property when it comes to multiplication. When students are struggling with 7×6, it is the distributive property that gives them the power to think $7 \times (3 + 3)$ or $(7 \times 3) + (7 \times 3)$ or $21 + 21$ or 42. Similarly, because the fives are usually well known, it is the distributive property that allows students to find 7×6 by thinking $(5 + 2) \times 6$ or 5 sixes plus 2 sixes or $30 + 12$ or 42. When connected to arrays and area models, the distributive law is another tool for reducing memory load and focusing on understanding.

Division and Properties

An important understanding with multiplication and division (as was the case with addition and subtraction) is that multiplication is commutative—the order of the factors does not matter. But, division is *not* commutative—12 divided by 2 is not at all the same as 2 divided by 12.

In addition, when dividing, it is important to note that there can be a time when there are not enough objects to make a set. For example, when dividing 5 by 6 and thinking how many groups of six are in five, students must understand that there are no groups of 6 in 5, but there are 5 left over.

Skip-Counting

Another important precursor to mastery of multiplication facts is skip-counting. Children have always counted by ones, twos, and fives, and soon discover that counting by twos results in multiples of two and counting by fives results in multiples of five. Knowing the sequence 2, 4, 6, 8, 10, 12, 14, 16, 18 . . . makes it easier to learn that 2×6 is 12 and 2×8 is 16. Similarly, cultural comfort with 5, 10, 15, 20, 25, 30, 35, 40, 45, 50 is one of the reasons that multiplying by five is rarely as taxing as multiplying by four or by six. Counting on by threes, fours, sixes, sevens, eights, and nines, though less common, gives students early access to these related multiplication facts. Asking students to count on by eights or back by sixes is a quick way to help build fluency at odd moments during the day.

Physical and Pictorial Representations

Another key way to develop numerical fluency with multiplication facts is through the use of arrays, rectangles of cubes, and area models. First, just visualizing 5×7 as shown in Figure 8.2 helps students see $5 \times 7 = 35$, $7 \times 5 = 35$, $35 \div 7 = 5$ and $35 \div 5 = 7$. But these representations also help students see that 5×7 is the same as $5 \times (5 + 2)$ which helps them see 5×7 as 25 plus 10.

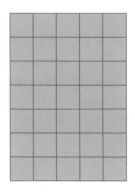

Figure 8.2
Rectangle model for 5 × 7

Key Fact Strategies

There are a broad range of strategies that students find essential for mastering multiplication facts with understanding rather than rote memorization.

The Doubles: Twos, Fours, and Eights; Threes and Sixes; Fives and Tens

Multiplying by twos has far-reaching effects for mathematics at all levels. Therefore it is very important that children see and experience all the facets of multiplying by two before memorizing the twos tables. Here are some key understandings about the twos.

1. All multiples of two are even numbers. Any even number can be divided by two (has two as a factor).
2. Two is the only even prime number, so all other primes are odd and all other even numbers are composite.
3. Multiplying by two is the same as doubling.
4. Multiples of two become multiples of four when doubled, so doubling $2 \times 3 = 6$ gets $4 \times 3 = 12$. And multiples of four become multiples of eight when doubled.

The twos double to create the multiples of four, and the fours double to create the multiples of eight. For example, knowing that 2×6 is twelve facilitates an understanding that 4×6 must be 12×2 or 24, and knowing that 4×8 is 32 facilitates understanding that 8×8 must be 32×2 or 64. Similarly, the threes double to create the multiples of six and the fives double to create the multiples of ten. As with all good mathematical teaching, instead of teachers presenting these as rules, students need to experience doubling, state the relationships using mathematical language, record them using arrays, and write the equations, before they can fully implement the information successfully in problem solving.

The blue dots in the array model in Figure 8.3 represent six rows of two or 6×2. The orange indicates what happens when you double 6×2 and create 6×4. Similar arrays can be built for all the multiples of four. Figure 8.4 represents the doubling of 6×4 to create and understand 6×8.

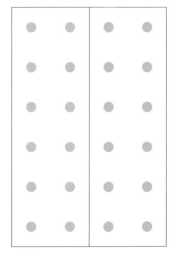

Figure 8.3 *Doubling 6×2 to get 6×4*

Figure 8.4 *Doubling 6×4 to get 6×8*

The Fives

And then there are the fives. As with the twos, teachers make assumptions that because children can count by fives, they already know their multiplicative relationships. This is not necessarily true; children may be able to count by fives to get an answer but not actually understand equal groups of five. They may also not understand the relative quantity of the product, but just say the last number in the pattern of counting by fives without really understanding why. It is thus very important for students to see and experience all of the facets of multiplying by five before memorizing any facts.

1. Fives are a part of life and appear in numerous places: five-minute span on the clock, five pennies in a nickel, five nickels in a quarter, five fingers, five toes, etc.

2. The multiples of five alternate odd and even. For example, $1 \times 5 = 5$ (odd) and $2 \times 5 = 10$ (even).

3. Five is also half of the pivotal number in our system, ten. Because of this special relationship, five has some other important features, such as its products being half of the products of ten.

4. Multiples of five have a zero or a five in the ones place. This is often taught as a divisibility rule, but seldom experienced. To watch the pattern unfold, make a chart of two columns and begin writing the multiples of five, as in Figure 8.5.

Look at five on the hundreds chart as well (see Figure 8.6). This helps children see the proportional relationship between five and ten and find patterns in their multiples.

Note that in this chart the multiples of five are colored orange, and the multiples of ten have a slash. What patterns do you see?

Tens	Ones
0	0
0	5
1	0
1	5
2	0
2	5
3	0
3	5
4	0
4	5

Figure 8.5
Patterns in multiples of five

1	2	3	4	5	6	7	8	9	10
11	12	13	14	15	16	17	18	19	20
21	22	23	24	25	26	27	28	29	30
31	32	33	34	35	36	37	38	39	40
41	42	43	44	45	46	47	48	49	50
51	52	53	54	55	56	57	58	59	60
61	62	63	64	65	66	67	68	69	70
71	72	73	74	75	76	77	78	79	80
81	82	83	84	85	86	87	88	89	90
91	92	93	94	95	96	97	98	99	100

Figure 8.6 *Multiples of five and ten in the hundreds chart*

Tens and Nines

The understanding that nine is one less than ten (see Pivotal Understanding 6 in Chapter 1) is expanded here to realize that nine is one less than one group of ten, two nines are two less than two groups of ten, and so on.

$1 \times 10 = 10$, so $1 \times (10 - 1) = 1 \times 9 = 9$ or $10 - 1$

$2 \times 10 = 20$, so $2 \times (10 - 1) = 2 \times 9 = 18$ or $20 - 2$

$3 \times 10 = 30$, so $3 \times (10 - 1) = 3 \times 9 = 27$ or $30 - 3$

$4 \times 10 = 40$, so $4 \times (10 - 1) = 4 \times 9 = 36$ or $40 - 4$

$5 \times 10 = 50$, so $5 \times (10 - 1) = 5 \times 9 = 45$ or $50 - 5$

$6 \times 10 = 60$, so $6 \times (10 - 1) = 6 \times 9 = 54$ or $60 - 6$

$7 \times 10 = 70$, so $7 \times (10 - 1) = 7 \times 9 = 63$ or $70 - 7$

$8 \times 10 = 80$, so $8 \times (10 - 1) = 8 \times 9 = 72$ or $80 - 8$

$9 \times 10 = 90$, so $9 \times (10 - 1) = 9 \times 9 = 81$ or $90 - 9$

$10 \times 10 = 100$, so $10 \times (10 - 1) = 10 \times 9 = 90$ or $100 - 10$

Building from Known Facts

When faced with a challenging or unknown fact, students can build from facts they already know. When finding 9×6, some students think that 5 nines is 45, but 6 nines must be 9 more or 54. Other students picture a 9×5 array and "see" an additional layer of 9 to help them see $45 + 9$. Still other students decompose the 9×6 into $9 \times (5 + 1)$ and use the distributive property to efficiently find $9 \times 5 + 9 \times 1$.

Keeping Track of Facts Mastered and Facts Not Yet Mastered

Figure 8.7 presents all 121 multiplication facts. Just like the equivalent table of addition facts presented and discussed in Chapter 5, this is a daunting amount of information and reminds us of how important it is to help students delimit what they may not know.

We use this chart as part of the discussion we have with students, like the one that opened this chapter. We use it to help students recognize that they really already know the thirty-three facts in the top three rows and the twenty-four remaining facts in the first three columns (shaded in purple in Figure 8.7). What

0 × 0	0 × 1	0 × 2	0 × 3	0 × 4	0 × 5	0 × 6	0 × 7	0 × 8	0 × 9	0 × 10
1 × 0	1 × 1	1 × 2	1 × 3	1 × 4	1 × 5	1 × 6	1 × 7	1 × 8	1 × 9	1 × 10
2 × 0	2 × 1	2 × 2	2 × 3	2 × 4	2 × 5	2 × 6	2 × 7	2 × 8	2 × 9	2 × 10
3 × 0	3 × 1	3 × 2	3 × 3	3 × 4	3 × 5	3 × 6	3 × 7	3 × 8	3 × 9	3 × 10
4 × 0	4 × 1	4 × 2	4 × 3	4 × 4	4 × 5	4 × 6	4 × 7	4 × 8	4 × 9	4 × 10
5 × 0	5 × 1	5 × 2	5 × 3	5 × 4	5 × 5	5 × 6	5 × 7	5 × 8	5 × 9	5 × 10
6 × 0	6 × 1	6 × 2	6 × 3	6 × 4	6 × 5	6 × 6	6 × 7	6 × 8	6 × 9	6 × 10
7 × 0	7 × 1	7 × 2	7 × 3	7 × 4	7 × 5	7 × 6	7 × 7	7 × 8	7 × 9	7 × 10
8 × 0	8 × 1	8 × 2	8 × 3	8 × 4	8 × 5	8 × 6	8 × 7	8 × 8	8 × 9	8 × 10
9 × 0	9 × 1	9 × 2	9 × 3	9 × 4	9 × 5	9 × 6	9 × 7	9 × 8	9 × 9	9 × 10
10 × 0	10 × 1	10 × 2	10 × 3	10 × 4	10 × 5	10 × 6	10 × 7	10 × 8	10 × 9	10 × 10

Figure 8.7 *Multiplication facts*

a relief to see a chart like this where we can check off fifty-seven of the 121 cells as *known* without much effort. Then we turn to the fifteen remaining facts that include 10 and that students also usually already know (shaded in purple) and thirteen remaining facts that include 5 (shaded in blue) and we're down to only thirty-six facts. But because of the commutative property, there are really only eighteen pairs of "troublesome" facts. Eight of these pairs involve threes and fours (shaded in yellow) and are supported by skip-counting, doubles, and adjusting already known facts. And that leaves what every teacher knows are the *big ten*: 6 × 6, 7 × 6, 8 × 6, 9 × 6, 7 × 7, 8 × 7, 9 × 7, 8 × 8, 9 × 8 and 9 × 9 (shaded in orange)!

Our job is to help students develop reliable strategies, like those discussed above, for each of these *big ten* and students are well on their way to overcoming the numerical fluency hurdle!

A Note about Division Facts

We have chosen to limit our discussion of multiplication and division facts to only multiplication for a simple reason. In our experience, there just aren't any division facts that need to be memorized. Rather, there are the inverses of multiplication facts that become division facts. Work with multiplication and division facts families generally suffices. Think about $63 \div 7$. Essentially no one stops and thinks that 63 divided by 7 is 9. Rather, our brains ask "What times 7 is 63?" and use the inverse multiplication fact to quickly compute the original division fact. Asking students to memorize more than 100 division facts when any of these facts is instantly retrievable from thinking about related multiplication facts just adds unnecessary and often debilitating memory load.

■ Classroom Activities

Once again, the following sample activities are provided as ideas for engaging students in the processes of contextualizing, constructing, representing, verbalizing, visualizing, and justifying. For each activity it is important to remember that eliciting explanations and justifications, and sometimes drawings, are key enablers of the development of fluency with multiplication and division facts.

Practice Games

High/Low

Materials needed:

> *one number cube with three 0s and three 1s on the faces*
>
> *one number cube with 1–6*
>
> *recording sheet and pencil*

This game allows for good practice multiplying by zero and one. The object of the game is to have the highest or lowest sum after ten tosses. Before the game begins, players must declare whether they are going for highest or lowest. Players can choose the same or different targets.

To begin the game, one player tosses the cubes and tells what they have. "I tossed a one and a one, so $1 \times 1 = 1$," for instance. Then the second player tosses the cube and says what they have. They each enter their results in the chart and move to the second round. After each round, they add their results from the previous rounds, and announce their running total. In the game shown in Figure 8.8, "You" won because 6 is less than 11. Note that if "Me" had played "high," both students would have won. Although this game seems quite easy, the endings are often a surprise, delighting the players.

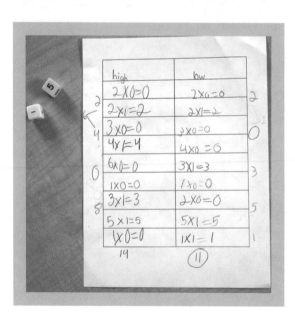

Figure 8.8 *Students playing High-Low*

Make the Product

In this game, use the game board shown in Figure 8.9 to find a path to reach a product of 12, 18, 24, 36, 48, or 64. Only horizontal and vertical moves are allowed (no diagonals). Student solutions allow for discussion about different paths, different factors, and which path or solution uses the fewest number of factors.

For example, to make a product of twelve using the game board shown, students might start at the 2 in the upper right corner, move down to 2 and then left to 3 to create a path of $2 \times 2 \times 3 = 12$. Alternatively, students might look at the second or third row and move from 4 to 3. See if you can find other paths to 12. Then try paths that result in 18.

1	2	1	2
2	4	3	2
2	4	3	2
1	2	1	2

Figure 8.9 *Grid for Make the Product*

Explorations

"Groups of . . . " Posters, Revisited

The "Groups of . . . " posters discussed in Chapter 7 continue to be useful as students learn to visualize, skip-count, and develop fluency with facts. For example, the Groups of Four poster is a wonderful stimulus for such questions as:

How many sides are on 7 squares?

How many legs are on 8 cows?

How many quarters are in $3?

Students should be expected to provide both an answer and an explanation of their thinking.

Multiplication Fact Patterns in the Hundreds Chart

There are many patterns that emerge from skip-counting on the hundreds chart, coloring in the different patterns, and conducting discussions about the patterns that emerge. Here are some of our favorite examples.

Figure 8.10 shows what happens when you color in the multiples of two. Here is how you might conduct the follow-up discussion:

What do you notice about multiples of two on the hundreds charts?

What do you notice about all the squares that are colored white?

Then you can move on to multiples of three. Here are some questions to support discussion of the products of three:

What do you notice about multiples of three on the hundreds chart?

What patterns do you see emerging? What do you notice about each diagonal?

1	2	3	4	5	6	7	8	9	10
11	12	13	14	15	16	17	18	19	20
21	22	23	24	25	26	27	28	29	30
31	32	33	34	35	36	37	38	39	40
41	42	43	44	45	46	47	48	49	50
51	52	53	54	55	56	57	58	59	60
61	62	63	64	65	66	67	68	69	70
71	72	73	74	75	76	77	78	79	80
81	82	83	84	85	86	87	88	89	90
91	92	93	94	95	96	97	98	99	100

Figure 8.10 *Multiples of three*

Division Patterns

Here is a simple activity that allows students to explore division by two and patterns with remainders. Ask students to divide the numbers from two to twenty by two.

$2 \div 2 = 1$

$3 \div 2 = 1 \text{ r}1$

$4 \div 2 = 2$

$5 \div 2 = 2 \text{ r}1 \ldots$

Ask students what they notice about the remainders when dividing by two. Why is it happening?

Now ask students to divide the numbers from three to thirty by three.

$3 \div 3 = 1$

$4 \div 3 = 1 \text{ r}1$

$5 \div 3 = 1 \text{ r}2$

$6 \div 3 = 2 \ldots$

Again, ask students what they notice about the remainders when dividing by three, and why the pattern occurs.

Continue with dividing four to forty by four, five to fifty by five, etc.

Chairs as Context

We suggested this activity in the previous chapter as an accessible way to strengthen an understanding of multiplication and division and what situations lend themselves to which operation. As we noted, since chairs are most often arranged in rows of an equal number of chairs, they serve as a good context for strengthening an understanding of multiplication and division (the previous chapter) *and* fact fluency (this chapter). Here are some questions that are helpful:

Chairs are arranged in rows. Each row has the same number of chairs:

4 rows, 7 chairs in each row. How many chairs in all? Explain your thinking.

Now, 48 chairs in all, arranged in 6 rows. How many chairs in each row? Explain your thinking.

This time, there are 30 chairs in all, 6 chairs in each row. How many rows? Explain your thinking.

Because the context is so accessible, this is a great place to have students create their own "chair" problems and share these problems with their partners. The chairs context also supports constructing and/or drawing pictures to represent the arrangements of chairs.

What's the Problem?

Another way to reinforce multiplication and division facts is to provide students with a single fact and ask them to create a problem that uses that fact, answer the problem, and explain how they know. Some teachers organize this activity with the chart shown in Figure 8.11.

Fact	Problem	Answer	Explanation
4 × 9	How many legs do 9 horses have?	36	I know that 4 × 10 is 40, so 4 × 9 must be four less or 36.
36 ÷ 9	I am sharing 36 stickers equally among 9 students. How many stickers will each student get?	4	I know that 9 × 4 is 36, so 36 divided by 9 must be 4.

Figure 8.11 *Examples for What's the Problem?*

Problem Bank

Here is a bank of word problems for multiplication and division facts that can be used to help students differentiate between multiplication situations and division situations, use different approaches to arrive at solutions, and model the situations. We strongly urge that teachers encourage multiple representations for each problem by asking students to draw a picture that represents the problem, create an appropriate number bond, write a number sentence, and then answer the problem in a complete sentence.

1. There are 3 bags of bouncing balls in the gym. In each bag, there are 4 balls. How many balls are in the gym?

2. Sarah bought ribbon for bows. She has 6 ribbons of 8 inches each. How many inches of ribbon did she buy?

3. Jason collected 40 seashells to share with his family. How many seashells will each person get if there are 5 people in Jason's family?

4. An art teacher has 36 ounces of clay. Each child in the class needs 4 ounces of clay to make a project. How many students will be able to make projects?

5. There are 21 students in a class. There are 7 students in each math group. How many groups of students will be in the class?

6. Crosby has 24 ounces of water in a jug. How many 4-ounce cups can he fill?

7. In the parade, the band marches in 9 rows with 6 players in each row. How many band members are in the parade?

8. Jerry's room is 8 feet by 7 feet. What is the area of the room in square feet?

9. Ira is preparing a display of bugs he caught. He has 18 bugs and he wants to put then in 3 rows. How many bugs will be in each row?

10. The area of the room is 72 square feet. If the room is 8 feet wide, what is its length?

11. For chorus, the music director arranged all 32 children in equal rows of 8 children. How many rows of children will there be?

12. A rectangle has an area of 56 inches. If two sides are each 8 inches long, what is the length of each of the other sides?

＊＊＊＊＊

It is almost impossible to overdo multiplication and division facts, given how often they arise in our everyday lives and what a waste of time and effort it is to turn to a calculator for what the brain can do far more quickly. But it is *how* fluency is developed that makes the difference.

Chapter 9

Developing Fluency Finding Products and Quotients

Other than fractions, which have their own special challenges, the two most common and frustrating "I-don't-get-it" separators of students are subtraction with regrouping and multiplying and dividing by two-digit numbers. We turn now to multi-digit multiplication and division. This topic, as every teacher is well aware, is the final instructional piece of whole number computation and makes use of nearly all the concepts and skills previously taught.

Key Ideas and Skills

Let's look at a problem and some different ways to solve it.

There are 22 classes at Newton School.

There are 25 children in each class.

In addition there are 2 teachers for each class.

Because of the school exit doors, the fire department limits the school to no more than 650 people.

Does the school's enrollment meet the fire department requirements?

Use words, numbers, and/or pictures to justify your answer.

It is wonderful when some students show us $25 + 2 = 27$ people $\times\, 22$ classes and multiply 27 by 22 to get 594 and announce that the school meets the requirements. It is just as wonderful when other students do their work mentally and tell us that they "know that $25 \times 2 = 50$ so $25 \times 20 = 500$ and two more 25s is 50, so my answer is 550 children and 44 teachers for a total of 594. So yes, they're fine." Or when others tell us that "Instead of multiplying 25 by 22, I can double the 25 and multiply it by 11 to get 550. With 44 teachers, that makes 594 so yes they meet the fire department requirements." Still others explain that "I know that 25×10 is 250 and there are two 10s in 22; so another 250 makes 500. There are still two 25s leftover which is 50, so the answer is 550 and 44. And still others immediately convert the problem to an array—either on paper or in their heads—with labels (as shown in Figure 9.1).

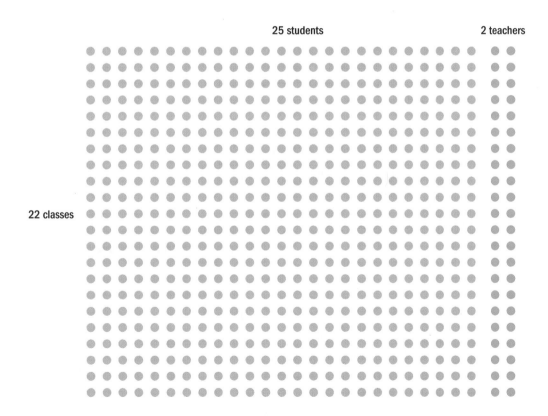

Figure 9.1 *Array model for 22 × (25 + 2)*

In each of these cases, students had to rely on lots of prior knowledge, underlying understanding, and numerical fluency. Some examples:

- Basic part-whole understandings (as discussed in Chapter 7)
- Adding to multiply (and, as we will see, subtracting to divide), including multi-digit addition and subtraction (see Chapter 6)
- Understanding the result of multiplying a whole number by 10, and later 100
- Understanding expanded notation and the distributive property: 22 is $20 + 2$, and 22×25 is the same as $(25 \times 20) + (25 \times 2)$
- The power of doubling or halving a number
- A working understanding of the commutative, associative, and distributive properties.

These powerful and underlying ideas support the development of needed fluency with multiplication and division of larger numbers and enable students to use a range of alternative approaches and different representations.

Within these broad concepts, there are several explicit understandings that support fluency with multi-digit multiplication and division.

Fact Knowledge

Having a fully retrievable working knowledge of multiplication and division facts to 10×10 obviously enhances one's ability to be successful with multi-digit multiplication and division. But when we speak of "fully retrievable" and a "working knowledge," we mean the ability to access these facts within two seconds—sometimes by memory, other times by visualization, and still other times via a strategy that works efficiently.

Place Value and Multiples of 10

Students need to understand place value, expanded notation, and the value of a number in its place. This is closely related to the ability to multiply any single digit by 10 and 100, and the understanding that 10×10 is 100. At its core, multiplication and division of larger numbers is built on a strong understanding of multiplying by multiples of 10. It is critical not just to know that 3×7 is 21, but also to be fluent in one's ability to find 30×7, 3×70, 30×70, 300×70, 30×700, and 300×700. These understandings become very helpful for recognizing that it just isn't reasonable, for instance, that $200 \times 20 = 4{,}000{,}000$.

Well-meaning teachers often offer rules like, "When you multiply by 10, just add a zero to the end of the number." The zero in the ones place certainly is the result of multiplying a number by 10, but we risk serious confusion when we suggest we are "adding a zero" as opposed to "appending a zero because it's ten times larger." (This can also cause confusion later when students begin working with decimals, where "adding a zero" does not necessarily change the value of the number!) Multiple experiences are necessary for children to totally grasp this concept.

Properties

Knowledge of the mathematical properties of multiplication and division (discussed in detail in Chapter 8) is also necessary. It is the associative property of multiplication that permits reasoning like: $6 \times 20 = 6 \times 10 \times 2 = 6 \times 2 \times 10 = 12 \times 10 = 120$. The distributive property allows students to break up problems using expanded notation. For example, the distributive property allows us to change 33×4 to $(30 + 3) \times 4$ to $(30 \times 4) + (3 \times 4)$ or $120 + 12$ for a product of 132. Similarly with division, it is the distributive property that allows us to change $318 \div 3$ to $(300 + 18) \div 3$ to $(300 \div 3) + (18 \div 3)$ or $100 + 6$ for a quotient of 106.

Friendly Numbers

The ability to use familiar or friendly numbers enhances one's ability to be flexible and solve problems mentally. Familiarity with multiples of 15, 25, 30, 50, and 75 can really assist children in solving multi-digit problems. For example, because four 25s is equal to 100, it is easy to multiply with other numbers close to 25. So for example, to find 26×32, think about twenty-five 32s. Since four 25s make 100, thirty-two 25s will make 800; one more 32 (because there are twenty-six 32s, not twenty-five) will make 832. Linked to this facility with familiar or friendly numbers is facility with estimation, an ability to judge the reasonableness of answers, and one's overall number sense.

Remainders

Students often develop misconceptions when we teach division *without* remainders first and then division *with* remainders later, under the guise of "it's easier for children that way." The truth is that, in real life, remainders exist at some times and not at others. In our considered opinion, it doesn't help students to learn first that remainders don't exist and then have them appear suddenly. Doing the problem 57 ÷ 3 first does not help improve the understanding needed to find 58 ÷ 3. We believe that from the outset children should learn to divide with and without remainders (and to interpret those remainders in problem contexts—see page 106 in Chapter 7) because they occur naturally and are a normal part of division.

Alternative Algorithms

As we said in Chapter 6, we reject the notion of "*the* standard algorithm" and believe that common sense argues for empowering our students with generalizable and efficient algorithms that may or may not be the so-called standard algorithm. This does *not* mean that we explicitly teach all of these alternative approaches, nor that we expect students to use or even understand them all. But when one algorithm is not making sense for a child, we have a responsibility to try to find an alternative that might, in fact, make a lot more sense and work with consistency and fluency. With just one algorithm, we hear a mindless mantra of "3×6 = 18 so put down the eight, carry the one, multiply again and add the one to the new product," or, in the case of division "daddy mother sister brother" or "divide multiply subtract bring down." Neither of these processes supports a meaningful understanding of why $25 \times 12 = 300$ or why $512 \div 30 = 17$ with a remainder of 2. Algorithms taught as mindless rules without understanding send debilitating long-term messages about what mathematics really is.

Figure 9.2 shows different approaches to multiplying a two-digit number by a one-digit number. Algorithm A represents the so-called standard or most traditional algorithm in the United States. Here we expect students to multiply 7 by 6 (ignoring that they are really multiplying 7 ones by 6 ones) and get 42, placing the 2 under the 7 and the 4, ideally a little smaller, above the 8. Next, students are supposed to multiply the 7 by 8, get 56, and add the 4 to get 60, for which the 0 is placed in the product and the 6 is placed above the 3, and so it goes with gigantic opportunity for confusion and for learning that mathematics is about following rules that make no sense, as opposed to a coherent sense-making process where one's actions can be explained.

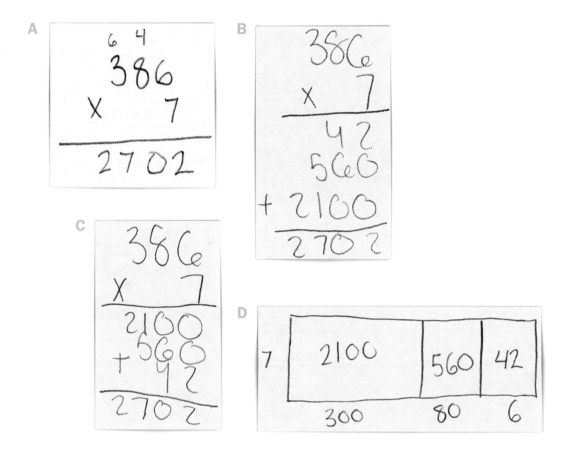

Figure 9.2 *There is more than one way to multiply, part 1*

Algorithms B and C, along with the bar model or expanded notation tape diagram in D, show a far more sensible partial products approach to multiplying numbers. In these partial products algorithms, instead of "7 × 6 is 42, so put the 2 down below the 7 and insert the 4 above the 8," students are expected to record that 7 × 6 is 42 and, lo and behold, the 42 goes exactly where the 42 ought to go. Next, students see 7 times 8 tens (or 80) and get a product of 560, which perfectly sensibly is recorded under the 42, and so on. The recording shown, moving from right to left in B and from left to right in C, aligns perfectly with the bar model and supports an understanding rarely attained with the standard algorithm.

Figure 9.3 expands the highly efficient partial products approach to multiplying two two-digit numbers, along with an area model.

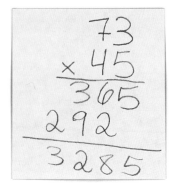
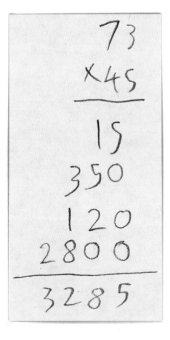
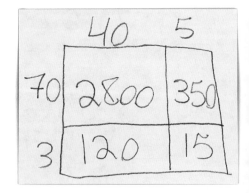

Figure 9.3 *There is more than one way to multiply, part 2*

Finally, Figure 9.4 shows a partial quotients approach to dividing by a one-digit divisor. We urge everyone to listen to themselves explaining how to use the standard "7 goes into 9 one time, so we put the 1 above the 9 and multiply 1 times 7 and subtract that 7 from the 9 to get 2, and then we bring down the 6 . . . " algorithm. Then try walking a student through the bar model and the recording of partial quotients shown in Figure 9.4. There is little doubt that for many students, the standard algorithm makes very little sense when compared with the partial quotients approach.

The Tricky Zero

Having only the standard algorithm can lead to serious misunderstanding when there is a zero in the middle of a multiplication or division problem. For example, consider 503×5. You multiply 5×3, put down the 5 and carry the 1. But then what? Do we skip the 0? Children often do not know how to continue. Figure 9.5 shows some common errors.

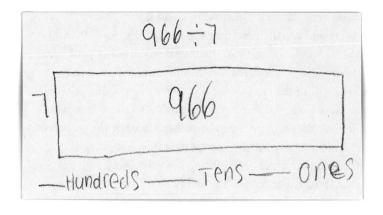
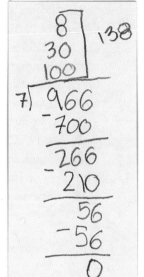
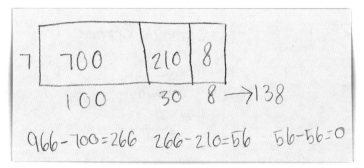

Figure 9.4 *An alternative approach to finding quotients*

CORRECT   Common Errors

$\overset{1}{5}03$ $\overset{1}{5}03$ $\overset{1}{5}03$
$\times\ \ 5$ $\times\ \ 5$ $\times\ \ 5$
─────   ─────   ─────
2515   265   2605

Figure 9.5 *Common errors multiplying with medial zero*

If students are able to think through the situation, though, they can think in terms of partial products and the distributive property: $503 \times 5 = (500 \times 5) + (3 \times 5) = 2500 + 15 = 2515$. Similarly, zeros in the middle of division problems can be nightmares of unrecognized errors (as shown in Figure 9.6). Consider, for example, 408 divided by 4. In the traditional algorithm, we would say four goes into four one time. Now since 4 doesn't go into 0, skip to the 8 into which 4 goes two times. Is it any wonder why so many students arrive at the incorrect answer of 12? Compare that to classrooms where reasonableness prevails and students think first, reasoning that there are 100 fours in 400 and 2 fours in 8 for a quotient of 102. Or that the answer couldn't possibly be 12 because 12 times 4 is 48—not even close to 408!

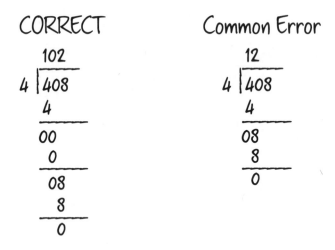

Figure 9.6 *Common error dividing with medial zero*

■ Classroom Activities

Once again, we suggest a range of classroom activities that are far removed from practice worksheets and that offer opportunities for incorporating the six processes of contextualizing, constructing, representing, verbalizing, visualizing, and justifying.

Place Value Review and Working with Multiples of 10

First to 500

This game provides practice with multiplying by 0, 1, and 10, builds understanding of multiples of 10, and reinforces key place value concepts.

> As with all games, we urge teachers to play the game with the whole class on the rug or with a document camera so that the students actually get to play the game and experience the rules before they play in pairs.

Materials: 2 cubes: One cube with 0, 1, 1, 10, 10, and 10; and another cube with 3, 5, 7, 8, 9, and 10

Base ten materials: ones-cubes, tens-rods, and hundred-flats

Base ten mat: fold a piece of 8.5 by 14 paper into three sections and label each column (hundreds, tens, and ones).

Hundreds	Tens	Ones

Player 1 tosses the two cubes, finds and announces the product of the two numbers, and takes place value materials matching that value. So if a player rolled 7 and 10, they would take 7 tens materials and say "I have seventy!" Then the next player takes a turn. After each round, students add up their total, announce this total, and record the total on the base ten mat. They can trade ones or tens for larger place value materials, but they should announce what they are doing as they do it (e.g., "I have 13 tens. I want 1 hundred and 3 tens."). The first to reach 500 wins.

List of 26

Divide the class into two teams. Write a group of 26 multiples of 10 on the board. Use both two- and three-digit multiples, up to 990.

Teams take turns. One person from a team chooses one number and defines it as a multiple of ten (e.g., "70 is 7 tens" or "120 is 12 tens"). If the number is described accurately, the team scores one point for a two-digit number and two points for a three-digit number. The opposing team records the equality (70 = 7 tens or 120 = 12 tens). The number is crossed off the list. When all the numbers are crossed off, the team with the most points wins and gets to make the next list of 26.

As students develop their understanding, expand the list to include four- and five-digit numbers, and require students to define the numbers in terms of both tens and hundreds (e.g., 2200 is 220 tens and 22 hundreds).

True or False

Provide students with sets of problems like these. For each, students should tell whether the equation is true or false and justify their answer. (You can also do this activity with other multiplication and division situations.)

Set 1:

1. $1000 \div 10 = 100$
2. $1500 \div 15 = 10$
3. $50 = 500 \div 100$
4. $10 = 10 \div 1$
5. $240 \div 24 = 10$
6. $990 \div 10 = 99$
7. $1050 \div 10 = 100$
8. $1100 \div 100 = 11$
9. $4800 \div 10 = 480$
10. $5000 \div 1000 = 5$

Set 2:

1. $10 \times 10 = 100$
2. $15 \times 10 = 1500$
3. $50 = 10 \times 50$
4. $10 = 1 \times 10$
5. $230 = 23 \times 1$
6. $99 \times 10 = 990$
7. $1050 = 15 \times 100$
8. $11 \times 10 = 1110$
9. $47 \times 100 = 4700$
10. $50 \times 100 = 5000$

Strike a Match!

Students match the numbers on the left to the expressions on the right and justify their answers. Encourage them to use their understanding of multiples of 10 in their justifications.

1. 700   a. $7 \times 7 \times 10$

2. 550   b. $2 \times 5 \times 5 \times 11$

3. 490   c. $5 \times 6 \times 10 \times 3 \times 3$

4. 630   d. $7 \times 2 \times 5 \times 10$

5. 720   e. $3 \times 3 \times 10 \times 7$

Building Knowledge of Multiples

Skip-Counting by Larger Numbers

Here are different ways to use skip-counting in your class. We encourage counting by 25s, 30s, 50s, 15s, and 75s, in that order, up to somewhere in the 300–500 range. Here are four possible variations.

1. Announce that as a class they will be counting by __s, in unison.

2. Count by __s individually by going around the room or a circle. If a student gets stuck, they can "call a friend" to help them out. This activity is intended for practice, not competition.

3. Count by ____ as a class, individually or in a small group, and stop periodically to ask, "How many ____s have we counted?" (Examples: *25, 50, 75, 100*. "How many 25s have we counted?" (4); and, continuing: *125, 150, 175, 200, 225*. "How many 25s now?" (9).)

4. Begin counting backwards by ____s from 500. Stop periodically to ask how many ___s you have counted.

Multiple Patterns

Make a three-column graph and fill in multiples of 25, 50, or 15 (for example), starting with zero (as in Figure 9.7). Ask students to talk about what they notice in the ones, tens, and hundreds places, and to explain why these patterns happen.

Page 142 Developing Numerical Fluency

Patterns for Multiples of 25				Patterns for Multiples of 50				Patterns for Multiples of 15		
H	T	0		H	T	0		H	T	0
				0	0	0				
0	0	0		0	5	0		0	1	5
0	2	5		1	0	0		0	3	0
0	5	0		1	5	0		0	4	5
0	7	5		2	0	0		0	6	0
1	0	0		2	5	0		0	7	5
1	2	5		3	0	0		0	9	0
1	5	0		3	5	0		1	0	5
1	7	5		4	0	0		1	2	0
2	0	0		4	5	0		1	3	5
2	2	5		5	0	0		1	5	0
								1	6	5
								1	9	0

Figure 9.7 *Multiple patterns*

Multi-Digit Multiplication Practice

Roll, Multiply, then Add

This game gives practice with multiplying the numbers 15, 25, and 30 times 1–6 and adding two- and three-digit numbers.

> *Materials needed: Two number cubes: one with 25, 25, 15, 15, 30, and 30, and the other with 1–6.*

Players take turns rolling two cubes and multiplying. They add the total to their previous total (or zero in the first round), and tell the multiplication equation. After ten turns, the player with the highest sum wins (see Figure 9.8).

Number Talks Using Expanded Multiplication

The following products are effective prompts for multiplication number talks. One solution for the first example is provided, but there are many different strategies that students can use to find these products.

25×40 $(20 + 5) \times 40 = (40 \times 20) + (40 \times 5) = 800 + 200 = 1000$

64×20

73×30

29×50

33×90

47×60

55×20

Figure 9.8 *Students playing Roll, Multiply, then Add*

Number Talks Using Expanded Division

The following products are effective prompts for division number talks. One solution for the first two examples is provided, but there are many different strategies that students can use to find these quotients.

$366 \div 3 = (300 \div 3) + (60 \div 3) + (6 \div 3) = 100 + 20 + 2 = 122$

$78 \div 4 = (40 \div 4) + (20 \div 4) + (18 \div 4) = 10 + 5 + 4\frac{1}{2}$ OR $10 + 5 + 4$ Remainder $2 = 19\frac{1}{2}$ or 19 remainder 2

$251 \div 2 =$

$725 \div 6 =$

$482 \div 12 =$

$1549 \div 14 =$

$2540 \div 22 =$

Problem Bank

Here is a bank of word problems for multiplication and division that can be used to help students differentiate between multiplication situations and division situations, use different approaches to arrive at solutions, and model the situations. As we have recommended with each of the previous problem banks, teachers should expect students to create a picture or drawing to represent the problem, create a number sentence that can be used to solve the problem, and write the answer in a complete sentence.

1. Robbie has 15 packages of candy. Each package has 20 candies. How many candies does Robbie have in all?

2. Sarah bought rope for a zip line. She has 8 hanks of rope. Each hank has 96 feet of rope. How much rope does Sarah have?

3. Mr. Wills shared $42 equally among his five children. How much money will each child receive?

4. The auditorium is set up with 24 rows of chairs. There are 18 chairs in each row. How many chairs are set up in the auditorium?

5. The principal asks the school custodian to set up 140 chairs in the multi-purpose room. The custodian places 20 chairs in each row. How many rows of chairs will be set up in the multi-purpose room?

6. Sam has one gallon of orange juice. That means he has 128 ounces of juice. How many 8-ounce cups can Sam fill?

7. The area of a rectangular living room is 192 square feet. The width of the living room is 8 feet. What is its length?

8. Rachel's grandfather's garden measures 32 feet by 9 feet. What is the area of the garden?

9. Ira is preparing a display of bugs he caught. He has 132 bugs and he wants to display them with 3 bugs on each poster. How many posters will Ira need?

10. Alexa made 5 batches of cookies. Each batch contains 18 cookies. How many cookies did Alexa make?

Pick-a-Number Games

As we noted in Chapter 6, we and our students are great fans of Pick-a-Number Games (see Figure 9.9), in which students place selected digits (0 to 9) in number spaces to get the largest products or quotients, smallest products or quotients, or a product or quotient closest to a given number. See Chapter 6, page 99, for a description of how to play. We use a variety of boards, starting with 2-digit by 1-digit multiplication, and including 2-digit by 2-digit and 3-digit by 2-digit multiplication, 2- and 3-digit by 1-digit division, and 3- and 4-digit by 2-digit division.

After students have played this game a few times, provide a new challenge. "Suppose we have picked the digits 4, 5 and 8. How could we put them on the game board so that their product is closest to 400?" This variation challenges students' estimation and mental computation skills.

Figure 9.9 *Pick-a-Number with multiplication*

* * * * *

As the culminating set of skills for whole number arithmetic, multiplication and division serve as temporary endpoints in the development of mathematical fluency, but they also serve as key pause points before these same ideas are applied to fractions and decimals and then to rates, proportions, and percents in grades 6 and 7. For these reasons, it is hard to imagine overemphasizing the development of fluency in multiplying and dividing whole numbers.

PART FOUR

Strategies for Creating a Schoolwide Culture of Fluency

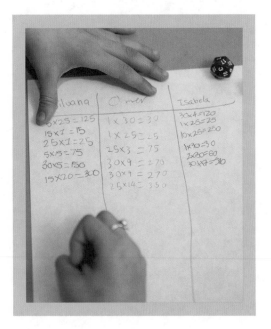

Chapter 10

*Activities and Resources
for Establishing a Culture of
Fluency and Fun*

In the previous chapters, we have introduced activities and ideas focused on specific areas of fluency. These activities work well in individual classrooms depending upon the mathematical topics being taught and the numerical fluency being developed. However, as part of creating a schoolwide culture of fluency, we urge teachers to turn as well to common activities that recur grade by grade and class by class from kindergarten to grade 5.

There are a range of fun, reasonably quick, often challenging and easy-to-use activities that can be adapted for use across grades. In addition, increasingly there are all sorts of accessible, easy-to-implement online resources that support this grade-by-grade development of fluency. In this chapter we identify and describe some of our favorites that can work as part of a schoolwide focus on numerical fluency.

Number Activities

24 Game

The 24 Game (www.24game.com) gives students 4 numbers that must be combined with operations to result in an answer of 24. Suppose that the four numbers are 4, 7, 8, and 8. Try to arrange these four numbers with parentheses and operation signs to get an answer of 24. Can you find a different solution? How about $(7 - (8 \div 8)) \times 4$ as one way to get 24?

We know teachers who keep and share the cards from various levels (easy to advanced) of the 24 Game in their classroom and give these challenges whenever there is down time in their classrooms.

One of us was recently in a school where the morning announcements end every day with "And now here are our two 24 challenges for the day. Ready? Challenge 1 uses *these* 4 numbers (announces 4 numbers) and Challenge 2 uses *these* 4 numbers (announces a different 4 numbers). Good thinking and have fun!" What a great way to build a school culture of fluency.

Can You Make 30 in 30 Ways?

In this activity you can select, or get your students to select, a number and then ask "Can you make 10 in ten ways?" or "Can you make 51 in fifty-one ways?" (Many teachers who track the number of days in school use the "day in school" as their number.) Answers are recorded on a poster for the class to see and monitor. This motivates students to be thinking about solutions throughout the day or days. There is only one rule to this activity: no two answers can be the same. However, many teachers like putting duplicate answers on one line so that participants always feel invited to respond, even if they turn out to have duplicated an earlier response.

Here is one possible set of responses for 30 ways to make 30:

1. $29 + 1 = 30$

2. $31 - 1 = 30$

3. $3 + 3 + 3 + 3 + 3 + 3 + 3 + 3 + 3 + 3 = 30$

4. $30 + 0 = 30$

5. $5 + 5 + 5 + 5 + 5 + 5 = 30$

6. $27 + 3 = 30$

7. $33 - 3 = 30$

8. 3 tens is 30

9. $28 + 2 = 30$

10. $90 - 60 = 30$

11. $25 + 5 = 30$

12. $50 - 20 = 30$

13. $5 \times 6 = 30$

14. $3 \times 10 = 30$

15. $(6 \times 4) + 6 = 30$

16. $(7 \times 4) + 2 = 30$

17. $(8 \times 3) + 6 = 30$

18. $(9 \times 3) + 3 = 30$

19. $(6 \times 6) - 6 = 30$

20. $100 - 70 = 30$

21. $90 \div 3 = 30$

22. $120 \div 4 = 30$

23. $(5 \times 4) + 10 = 30$

24. $(8 \times 5) - 10 = 30$

25. $1 + 1 + 1 + 1 + 1 + 2 + 2 + 2 + 2 + 3 + 3 + 3 + 4 + 4$

26. $(20 \times 2) - 10 = 30$

27. $(99 \div 3) - 3 = 30$

28. $(100 \div 2) - 20 = 30$

29. $(7 \times 3) + 9 = 30$

30. $(120 \div 3) - 10 = 30$

Four Fours

The Four Fours task is to use exactly four 4s to form every whole number from 0 to 50 using only the operation signs $+, -, \times, \div$, parentheses, and, when students get to third or fourth grade, you can add ! (factorial). ($4! = 4 \times 3 \times 2 \times 1 = 24$ and $5! = 5 \times 4 \times 3 \times 2 \times 1$ or 120), so things can get really interesting. For example, you can make:

$$0 = 44 - 44$$

$$1 = (4 \div 4) \times (4 \div 4)$$

$$2 = (4 \div 4) + (4 \div 4)$$

$$3 = (4 + 4 + 4) \div 4$$

Now, can you make every other integer to 50?

We have seen teachers start with three 3s and challenge older students with how many different numbers between 0 and 100 they can get with five 5s!

Guess My Number

Guess My Number is a wonderful classroom game to encourage number sense and numerical fluency. The object of the game is not just to guess one person's number, but also to be able to write clues for one's own secret number. It is much easier to guess a number than to prepare questions for someone else to answer. This makes this activity low entry, high ceiling, because anyone can ask questions, while those who are ready for a challenge can work to create tricky puzzles of their own. Here are a few examples:

My number is more than 10 and less than 16.

My number can be made with three groups of 5.

My number is the same as 1 more than 14.

What is my number?

My number is greater than 1000 and less than 1100.

My number is odd.

You say my number when you count by 5s in the thousands.

My number has a 4.

Guess my number!

If you divide me by 2, your remainder is 1.

If you divide me by 3, your remainder is 1.

If you divide me by 4, your remainder is 1.

If you divide me by 5, your remainder is 0.

If you divide me by 6, your remainder is 1.

My number is less than 30.

Guess my number!

When students begin writing their own, you may want to give them a constraint, such as having the number be less than 50. When students first write their own clues, often the clues are really answers, or there are not enough clues. Tightening one of these problems up and making sure it makes sense is a worthwhile challenge for all students.

Money Activities

Making Change

Look at the fluency-building possibilities of making change. All you need to do is identity the amount of change and the available coins and challenge students to find all the different ways to make that amount with those coins. Figure 10.1 is an example for making 55 cents with nickels, dimes, and quarters.

Amount	Nickels	Dimes	Quarters
55 cents	11	0	0
55 cents	9	1	0
55 cents	7	2	0
55 cents	5	3	0
55 cents	3	4	0
55 cents	1	5	0
55 cents	2	2	1
55 cents	4	1	1
55 cents	6		1
55 cents	1		2
55 cents		3	1

Figure 10.1 *Making change*

You can deepen the discussion with questions like:

What patterns do you see?

When there are no quarters, why are there an odd number of nickels?

When there is one quarter, why is there an even number of nickels?

Does 5 nickels and 3 dimes equal 3 dimes and one quarter? Can you prove it?

All this takes is the question, "Which coins are we using?" and letting students decide among pennies, nickels, dimes, quarters, and even half-dollars. Follow up with "How much change do you get?" and the students can name an amount. To add some incentive to the activity, we love to ask students first to guess how many different ways they think there will be. The final tables are almost always opportunities to find and discuss patterns.

What Could You Have Purchased?

SALE

Pencils 7¢

Pens 8¢

Erasers 9¢

Figure 10.2 *Price list*

Students are very familiar with computing the cost of orders, given menus or price lists. For example, traditional word problems might include (see price list shown in Figure 10.2) how much will 4 pencils, 5 pens and 2 erasers cost and how much change would you get from $1?

Far more interesting and challenging are the non-routine problems that emerge when this is reversed and the question becomes "If you spent exactly 83¢ in this store, what could you have purchased? How many different ways could you spend exactly 83¢ in this store?" Students are often amazed to find that there are more than ten different orders that all result in a total cost of 83¢.

Online Resources

Which One Doesn't Belong? (www.wodb.ca)

Christopher Danielson and Mary Bourassa are the creators of the increasingly popular "Which One Doesn't Belong?" This routine can induce great thinking and excitement. Students are presented with four numbers or four objects or four shapes and are expected to decide which one they think doesn't belong and to justify their choice. There is no one right answer! There can be a valid explanation for why each of the four might not belong with the other three. In fact, the beauty of this routine is that in each case, an argument can be made that each item has a good reason *not* to belong, and for many of the numbers or shapes, there is more than one reason why it might not belong. Figure 10.3 is one example.

Children might say that:

> The "one pip" doesn't belong because it is the only one that is not five.
>
> The "5" doesn't belong because it is the only numeral.
>
> The "small white five pips" doesn't belong because it is the only one that is small.
>
> The "blue die" doesn't belong because it is the only one that is blue.

Figure 10.3 *Which one doesn't belong?*

And they can get a lot trickier and a lot more challenging. For example, Figure 10.4 is one that we leave for you to figure out. After some practice and experience, students can make up their own Which One Doesn't Belong game boards.

Estimation 180 (www.estimation180.com)

Sometimes nothing more than a picture stimulates the kinds of thinking and estimating that we seek for all students. Andrew Stadel's wonderful Estimation 180 website contains more than 200 opportunities for students to make estimates, identify estimates they think are too high or too low, and justify these various estimates.

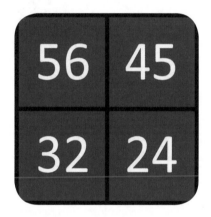

Figure 10.4 *Which one doesn't belong?*

Here's an example of how we've seen Estimation 180 play out in a classroom. Students are presented with the picture in Figure 10.5 and are asked to estimate the height of the Ferris wheel and justify their estimate. The protocol Stadel recommends is to ask students for an estimate they know must be too low and an estimate they know must be too high. Then, using these two extremes, propose a reasonable estimate. In addition to the numerical fluency being reinforced, these Estimation 180 mini-tasks reinforce measurement and pre-proportional reasoning understandings.

Figure 10.5 *How tall is the ride?*

Number Mobiles (https://solveme.edc.org/Mobiles.html)

Another resource that we have seen to thoroughly engage students is the SolveMe number mobile puzzles from EDC.

The website provides 134 puzzles at the explorer, puzzler, and master levels that can be used as part of algebraic thinking and numerical fluency from grade 2 (the easy ones) through middle school (see Figure 10.6). In these puzzles, students must make the scale balance by determining the value of each shape. The interface lets them drag "strings" from the mobile to form matching equations, replace equivalent quantities, and otherwise manipulate the mobile as they solve.

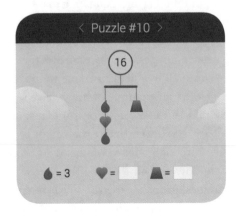

Figure 10.6 *Mobile puzzle*

Would You Rather (www.wouldyourathermath.com)

Another online resource that teachers and students find helpful for linking problem solving and numerical fluency is the set of Would You Rather choices that students need to decide between. See Figure 10.7 for one of many such decisions students need to make and justify.

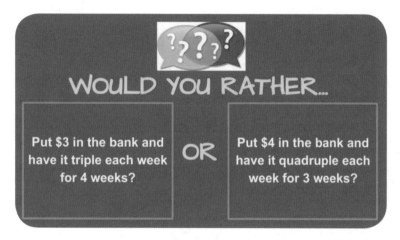

Figure 10.7 *Would you rather . . . ?*

* * * * * * * * * *

The schoolwide collaborative structures discussed in the next chapter are perfect opportunities for sharing how these activities and resources have worked and how they can be adapted to be consistent, cross-grade features of mathematics instruction and fluency development throughout a school.

Chapter 11

It Takes a School to Develop Numerical Fluency

We wrap things up with a bit of professional honesty: changing instructional practice in the ways advocated in this book is hard!

Moving from merely gathering answers to expecting explanations and justifications requires a mindset shift that takes time and support to emerge. Moving from the convenience of worksheets to the complexities of eliciting and celebrating the thinking that accompanies alternative approaches to finding solutions is often a difficult transition. But we can't just make these changes in the "good" teachers' classrooms. For change to stick, we need to create a school culture focused on the purposeful development of numerical fluency as an integral part of K–5 mathematics in every classroom and among all students regardless of labels, languages, or learning needs.

The levels of fluency discussed in this book cannot be developed in a single lesson or a single classroom or even over the course of a single year. Instead, supporting the growth from parts and wholes to sums and differences to products and quotients takes a schoolwide commitment that is infused into every classroom and every pull-out program where mathematics is taught. It takes a shared understanding of exactly what numerical fluency is and what common classroom routines and practices support its development. And it takes a shared sense that what happens in grade x directly impacts what can be done in grade $x + 1$.

There are a range of strategies that schools can and must adopt to develop this schoolwide culture and commitment. We advocate for serious consideration and implementation of the following collaborative structures to build this knowledge, culture, and commitment.

Making Better Use of Meetings

The heart of every coherent, equitable and effective mathematics program is the consistency of daily high quality instruction that emerges, in part, from professional interactions that occur during grade-level planning meetings. The philosophy of "you do your thing and I'll do my thing" too often shortchanges students and severely complicates matters for the teachers who will face these students next year. Making better use of grade-level and whole-school faculty meetings can help.

Grade-Level Meetings

Teachers tell us that their grade-level planning meetings are essential sharing and problem-solving experiences that strengthen the skill and knowledge of all participants. Starting with a goal of developing numerical fluency appropriate for that grade level for every student and acknowledging that worksheets, "mad minute drills," and mindless practice are inappropriate strategies for meeting that goal, grade-level meetings are where teachers use resources like the ideas presented in this book and collaboratively develop lessons that incorporate the processes and pivotal understandings we have discussed.

Consider the one-hour meeting of three first-grade teachers all wrestling with the challenge of developing fluency with addition and subtraction facts. They know that their students need a stronger sense of appropriate strategies and they know that their students need to support their answers with justifications that explain the various strategies they use. Figure 11.1 shows the "strategy chart" they develop to post and use in each of their classrooms:

Faculty and Cross-Grade Meetings

More and more teachers tell us that the focus of faculty meetings is shifting from administrivia and announcements (easily conveyed by e-mail) to teaching and learning throughout the school. As part of this transition, faculty meetings become powerful opportunities for presentation of model lessons, schoolwide discussions of the shifts in practice required to strengthen numerical fluency, video analysis, analysis of student work, and celebrations of success. The question for teachers, coaches, and administrators is simple: Why bemoan an absence of needed fluency when small, universally implemented shifts can make such a difference? And why not use faculty meetings to address these shifts and build expectations that they will be widely implemented?

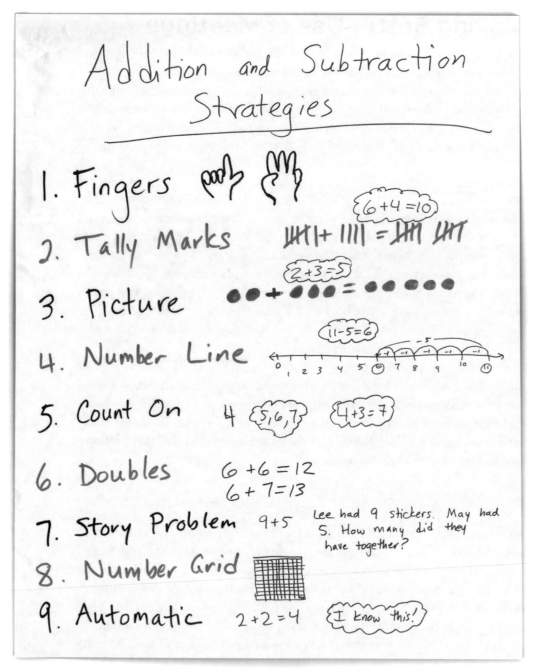

Addition and Subtraction Strategies

1. Fingers

2. Tally Marks   ШШ + |||| = ШШ ШШ $6+4=10$

3. Picture   ●● + ●●● = ●● ●●● $2+3=5$

4. Number Line $11-5=6$

5. Count On   4 5,6,7 $4+3=7$

6. Doubles $6+6=12$
             $6+7=13$

7. Story Problem $9+5$ Lee had 9 stickers. May had 5. How many did they have together?

8. Number Grid

9. Automatic $2+2=4$ I know this!

Figure 11.1 *Strategy chart*

Using Video

Because most of the practices that develop numerical fluency cannot be done with worksheets or via independent student work, video is often the most useful vehicle for capturing the discourse, engagement, and teaching moves found in great lessons. When we use video clips as part of grade-level meetings or faculty meetings, we limit clips to no more than ten minutes and almost never let a video run for more than three minutes without pausing for discussion. In our experience, the video is a stimulus for discussion and a chance to envision what is possible in a real classroom in our own school with one of our own teachers. We tend to guide this discussion with only three questions:

- What was impressive in what you observed? Why was that impressive and why do you think it worked for students?
- What questions do you have about the teaching and the learning in the lesson we observed? What might you do differently?
- On the basis of the video and our discussion, what one or two shifts are you willing to commit to making in your own class to better serve your students?

Consider a third-grade teacher who uses a number talk model to do an estimation task near the beginning of every mathematics lesson. How hard is it to capture the eight minutes of instruction on video using a phone or tablet? How hard is it to view, rewind, and review section by section such a video during a faculty meeting? And how hard is it to use the video to stimulate discussion of what is going on, how it is effective, and what would prevent the entire faculty from adopting such a practice?

The key for this and other approaches to work is to start small. Use volunteers who are willing to take a risk. Ensure a safe and respectful space for discussion. Focus, in the end, on the one or two changes that teachers are willing to commit to making.

Teacher Collaboration

Beyond these larger-scale meetings, teachers also need ways to collaborate directly.

Combining Classes

It is not at all uncommon to find very diverse comfort levels with teaching mathematics among grade-level colleagues. We have seen teachers combine their classes and co-teach the larger group for the purpose of modeling and encouraging strategies that need to be practiced in all classes. Teachers tell us that they marvel at what their own students are able to do when working with a broader pool of students and under the guidance of another teacher. Seeing this change in behavior and engagement is the best motivator to incorporate these instructional shifts back in one's own classroom.

Collegial Visits

It astounds us both how rarely teachers get to observe each other—not because of a lack of time, but because collegial visits just aren't part of most school cultures. But when we hear how instructional practices were reinforced because someone saw them in a colleague's class or when we are told how one collegial observation "completely changed how I'm introducing multiplication to my students," we realize how valuable and underutilized this collaborative structure is. In all seriousness, we ask, how hard is it to schedule some collegial visits as part of the agenda for grade-level meetings? How hard is it to take a music period or gym period once a month to wander into a colleague's class? Whether done informally or more formally to see a specific strategy or lesson, we find classroom visits invaluable. In our experience, once-a-month collegial visits, far from being burdens, are powerful and exciting learning opportunities that come at essentially no cost.

Consider how two fifth-grade teachers can agree to reschedule their math block to facilitate each teacher being able to observe a math lesson on a topic of common concern while their students are in music or art. Consider that power of the end-of-the-day discussion about "what you did and what I did" and what seemed to work and why, as well as what didn't seem to work as well and why. Consider how something this simple breaks down silos of isolation that make growth and improvement so much more difficult.

Coaching

In our experiences, little is as effective as real time coaching/co-teaching with individual teachers and their students. Effective coaching is not sitting in the back of the room taking notes, but rather active involvement in the lesson, focused on a specific instructional practice, accompanied by the all-important post-lesson debrief. This is not the place to describe effective coaching practices, but it is the place to remind us that shifting practice and mindsets is not easy and unlikely to be done in isolation. Consistent coaching is one more powerful way to gradually create a schoolwide commitment to the development of numerical fluency.

Garnering Administrative Support

If you are a teacher reading this, it is the perfect opportunity to copy this chapter and share it with your principal. If you are an administrator reading this, you know that many of these collaborative structures require your support and encouragement.

Some strategies for providing the leadership necessary to support these activities include:

- Minimizing spending meeting time on administrivia that can be disseminated by e-mail and maximizing focus on teaching and learning.

- Participating in grade-level meetings to provide ongoing support and encouragement for sharing around issues of teaching and learning.

- Working with a few volunteers to videorecord mathematics lessons that incorporate the development of fluency, and using these videos for faculty meeting viewing and discussion.

- Encouraging and supporting a schoolwide commitment to collegial observations that create a much stronger "we're all in this together" culture. Just as our students learn from each other, as educators, we have our colleagues as the first line of support in doing more and better on behalf of our students.

In short, the development of universal numerical fluency is *not* rocket science. But neither is it easy. We have tried to set down a set of pivotal understandings and key instructional processes that we know support the effective development of numerical fluency. We have tried to present a wide array of examples of what our mathematics lessons need to incorporate. And we've closed with a plea for collaboration and a schoolwide focus.

We urge you to go forth and start small. We urge you to begin with what seems simple. We urge you to then build on these initial efforts. We urge you to monitor what works and what doesn't. And we urge you to remember that when *every* child leaves your classroom confident in their numerical fluency—because of what *you* have done—you change the world for that student, for every student, and for our collective good. Why else would we as teachers do what we do?

Appendix

Addition and Subtraction Situations[1]

	Result Unknown	Change Unknown	Start Unknown
Add to	Two bunnies sat on the grass. Three more bunnies hopped there. How many bunnies are on the grass now? $2 + 3 = ?$	Two bunnies were sitting on the grass. Some more bunnies hopped there. Then there were five bunnies. How many bunnies hopped over to the first two? $2 + ? = 5$	Some bunnies were sitting on the grass. Three more bunnies hopped there. Then there were five bunnies. How many bunnies were on the grass before? $? + 3 = 5$
Take from	Five apples were on the table. I ate two apples. How many apples are on the table now? $5 - 2 = ?$	Five apples were on the table. I ate some apples. Then there were three apples. How many apples did I eat? $5 - ? = 3$	Some apples were on the table. I ate two apples. Then there were three apples. How many apples were on the table before? $? - 2 = 3$

	Total Unknown	Addend Unknown	Both Addends Unknown
Put Together/ Take Apart	Three red apples and two green apples are on the table. How many apples are on the table? $3 + 2 = ?$	Five apples are on the table. Three are red and the rest are green. How many apples are green? $3 + ? = 5, 5 - 3 = ?$	Grandma has five flowers. How many can she put in the red vase and how many in her blue vase? $5 = 0 + 5, 5 = 5 + 0$ $5 = 1 + 4, 5 = 4 + 1$ $5 = 2 + 3, 5 = 3 + 2$

	Difference Unknown	Bigger Unknown	Smaller Unknown
Compare	("How many more?" version): Lucy has two apples. Julie has five apples. How many more apples does Julie have than Lucy? ("How many fewer?" version): Lucy has two apples. Julie has five apples. How many fewer apples does Lucy have then Julie? $2 + ? = 5, 5 - 2 = ?$	(Version with "more"): Julie has three more apples than Lucy. Lucy has two apples. How many apples does Julie have? (Version with "fewer"): Lucy has 3 fewer apples than Julie. Lucy has two apples. How many apples does Julie have? $2 + 3 = ?, 3 + 2 = ?$	(Version with "more"): Julie has three more apples than Lucy. Julie has five apples. How many apples does Lucy have? (Version with "fewer"): Lucy has 3 fewer apples than Julie. Julie has five apples. How many apples does Lucy have? $5 - 3 = ?, ? + 3 = 5$

[1] Adapted from Box 2-4 of *Mathematics Learning in Early Childhood*, National Research Council (2009, pp. 32, 33).

Multiplication and Division Situations

	Unknown Product	Group Size Unknown ("How many in each group?" Division)	Number of Groups Unknown ("How many groups?" Division)
	$3 \times 6 = ?$	$3 \times ? = 18$, and $18 \div 3 = ?$	$? \times 6 = 18$, and $18 \div 6 = ?$
Equal Groups	There are 3 bags with 6 plums in each bag. How many plums are there in all? *Measurement example.* You need 3 lengths of string, each 6 inches long. How much string will you need altogether?	If 18 plums are shared equally into 3 bags, then how many plums will be in each bag? *Measurement example.* You have 18 inches of string, which you will cut into 3 equal pieces. How long will each piece of string be?	If 18 plums are to be packed 6 to a bag, then how many bags are needed? *Measurement example.* You have 18 inches of string, which you will cut into pieces that are 6 inches long. How many pieces of string will you have?
Arrays, Area	There are 3 rows of apples with 6 apples in each row. How many apples are there? *Area example.* What is the area of a 3 cm by 6 cm rectangle?	If 18 apples are arranged into 3 equal rows, how many apples will be in each row? *Area example.* A rectangle has area 18 square centimeters. If one side is 3 cm long, how long is a side next to it?	If 18 apples are arranged into equal rows of 6 apples, how many rows will there be? *Area example.* A rectangle has area 18 square centimeters. If one side is 6 cm long, how long is a side next to it?
Compare	A blue hat costs $6. A red hat costs 3 times as much as the blue hat. How much does the red hat cost? *Measurement example.* A rubber band is 6 cm long. How long will the rubber band be when it is stretched to be 3 times as long?	A red hat costs $18 and that is 3 times as much as a blue hat costs. How much does a blue hat cost? *Measurement example.* A rubber band is stretched to be 18 cm long and that is 3 times as long as it was at first. How long was the rubber band at first?	A red hat costs $18 and a blue hat costs $6. How many times as much does the red hat cost as the blue hat? *Measurement example.* A rubber band was 6 cm long at first. Now it is stretched to be 18 cm long. How many times as long is the rubber band now as it was at first?
General	$a \times b = ?$	$a \times ? = p$ and $p \div a = ?$	$? \times b = p$, and $p \div b = ?$

References

Boaler, Jo. 2016. *Mathematical Mindsets*. San Francisco, CA: Jossey-Bass.

Carpenter, Thomas, E. Fennema, M.L. Franke, L. Levi, and S.B. Empson. 1999. *Children's Mathematics: Cognitively Guided Instruction*. Portsmouth, NH: Heinemann.

Clements, Douglas H. 1999. "Subitizing: What Is It? Why Teach It?" *Teaching Children Mathematics* 5 (7): 400–405.

Fuson, Karen, and Sybilla Beckmann. 2012. "Standard Algorithms in the Common Core State Standards." *NCSM Journal* (Fall/Winter 2012-2013): 14–30. Retrieved from: www.mathedleadership.org/docs/resources/journals /NCSMJournal_ST_Algorithms_Fuson_Beckmann.pdf.

National Council of Teachers of Mathematics. 2000. *Principles and Standards for School Mathematics*. Reston, VA.

_____. 2014. *Principles to Actions: Ensuring Mathematical Success for All*. Reston, VA.

National Governors Association Center for Best Practices, Council of Chief State School Officers. 2010. *Common Core State Standards for Mathematics*. Washington, DC: Council of Chief State School Officers and National Governors Association.

Parker, Ruth, and Cathy Humphreys. 2015. *Making Number Talks Matter: Developing Mathematical Practices and Deepening Understanding, Grades 4–10*. Portland, ME: Stenhouse.

Parrish, Sherry. 2010. *Number Talks: Helping Children Build Mental Math and Computation Strategies, Grades K–5*. Sausalito, CA: Math Solutions.

Ray-Riek, Max. 2013. *Powerful Problem Solving*. Portsmouth, NH: Heinemann.

U.S. Census. 2010. "List of Largest Cities in Nebraska by Population." https://en.wikipedia.org/wiki/List_of_cities_in_Nebraska.